ORNAMENTAL CONIFERS

The new compact study guide and identifier

IDENTIFYING

ORNAMENTAL CONIFERS

The new compact study guide and identifier

Richard Bird

CHARTWELL
BOOKS, INC.

A QUINTET BOOK

Published by Chartwell Books
A Division of Book Sales, Inc.
PO Box 7100
Edison, New Jersey 08818–7100

This edition produced for sale in the U.S.A., its
territories and dependencies only.

ISBN 0–7858–0324–6

This book was designed and produced by
Quintet Publishing Limited
6 Blundell Street
London N7 9BH

Creative Director: Richard Dewing
Designer: James Lawrence
Editor: Helen Varley
Photographer: Richard Bird

Typeset in Great Britain by
Central Southern Typesetters, Eastbourne
Manufactured in Singapore by Bright Arts Pte Limited
Printed in Singapore by Star Standard Industries Pte Limited

CONTENTS

INTRODUCTION

. . . .

WHAT IS A CONIFER?

A conifer can be simply defined as a plant that bears cones. Unfortunately this is not the whole story as some, such as the yews, do not bear recognizable cones, but something more akin to a fruit. A fuller explanation is that the conifers are members of the Gymnospermae, which is a class of plant that bears naked seed, as opposed to the rest of the seed-bearing plants that carry their seed within an ovary.

There are three botanical orders within the Gymnospermae that make up the conifers, namely the Coniferales (which includes the cone-bearing plants), Taxales (which includes the yews) and the Ginkgoales (which includes the ginkgo).

CLASSIFICATION

The three orders above are divided up into families, genera, species, and finally varieties and cultivars. The families are broad groups of genera that have certain characteristics in common. For example, there is the family Pinaceae, all members of which have narrow, needlelike leaves that grow in clusters, each cluster forming

A B O V E : Young pine cones.

A B O V E : Larch cones and leaves.

a cylinder. The families are split up into genera, which consist of all the plants that have many common characteristics. For example, within the Pinaceae there are the genera *Pinus,* the pines, and *Larix,* the larches. Within each genus are individual species, the basic unit of classification. For example, within the genus *Pinus,* there is *Pinus sylvestris,* the Scots pine.

Individual species can vary in the wild and in cultivation, in height, shape and colour. A form that is distinct in one of these respects is given an individual name. If discovered in the wild it is known as a variety, and if of garden origin it is called a cultivar. Cultivar names are in single quotes: *Pinus sylvestris* 'Beuvronensis'.

ANATOMY

The structure of conifers is the same as that of any other trees. They are mainly single-stemmed trees, but some throw up several main stems, creating a bush-like structure. The bark is in two layers, the outer being a protective one. In some, such as *Sequoia,* the bark is fibrous and thick to protect the tree against fire. In young trees the bark is generally smooth, but it roughens as the tree ages.

Most but not all conifers are evergreen; larch *Larix* is one of the most obvious exceptions. The leaves vary considerably, but are generally distinct from other types of tree and shrub. The majority are needle like; long and narrow. Sometimes they

A B O V E : Young pine growth.

are pointed, sometimes blunt. Sometimes they are round in section, sometimes flattened. Some have strange structures. For example, each cluster of pine leaves grows out of a sheath, making up a cylinder if you press them all together, each leaf being a segment of the circle.

Other leaves are more like scales. These are short, flat leaves that clasp and often hide the shoot on which they are growing. The cypresses are a good example. When leaves are held tightly against the stem they are said to be adpressed. Leaves are carried in several different ways in conifers. In some they are held in clusters, in others they grow spirally round a stem. In the latter they may grow out like a brush or they may have a "parting", so they appear to grow in two rows on either side of the shoot. The *Ginkgo* is the only conifer to have broad leaves, similar to other non-coniferous trees.

In the wild, most conifers have green foliage. Some change colour at the onset of winter. The cryptomerias, for example, frequently take on a purple or bronze hue. In cultivation a wide range of foliage colours has been bred, usually starting from plants that have sported (thrown up aberrant shoots, often of a different colour) either in the wild or in cultivation. Golden foliage is particularly popular. Sometimes the leaves are totally coloured, and at others they are only partially so, giving a variegated look to the tree.

A B O V E : Pine flowers.

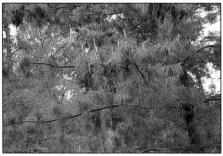

A B O V E : Pine cones. *T O P : Young cones.*

FLOWERS AND CONES

The flowers on conifers are the young cones. Male and female sex organs are carried in separate flowers; in many other flowering plants they are combined in one flower. In most conifers the male and female cones are carried on the same plant, but some genera, such as yews, junipers and monkey puzzles, are dioecious, that is, the male and female flowers are carried on separate plants. If you want mature seeding cones of this type of conifer, you will need a male and a female plant.

The male cones produce the pollen and the females the seed. The pollen is dispersed by the wind. Fertilization in some species takes a long time, a full year in the pines. Male cones are often on the lower branches, the female ones on the upper, stronger growths. The female cones consist of two types of scale: the outer, sterile ones which form the case; and an inner one which carries the seed. The shape and form of the scales determine the shape of the cone. The length of time taken for the seed to mature varies, but it can take up to three years in a pine.

A B O V E : Cones of *Tsuga heterophylla.*

When ripe, the cones open and the seeds are dispersed on the wind. In some cases it needs hot weather or even a fire to achieve this. A tree may carry its ripe cones for 20 years or more before a fire clears the ground of vegetation, which will give the falling seed the advantage of no competition when it germinates. Some cones disintegrate on the trees, making them of no use as house decorations. Others stay whole, with the outer bracts simply opening rather than falling off.

The seed of the yews is carried in a fleshy fruit. The structure is botanically similar to a cone. The seed is usually dispersed by birds eating fruit and then evacuating the undigested seed some distance from the parent plant. Juniper has fleshy fruit but it is more recognizable as a cone.

Cones vary considerably in shape and colour. In some plants they are a prominent feature. In others they are insignificant.

GROWTH

Many of the conifers in cultivation are derived from wild plants, while others are of garden origin. Dwarf and miniature forms have usually been created by taking shoots from the tight balls of the slow-growing "witches'-brooms" and grafting them onto a cultivated stock. "Witches'-brooms" are abnormal growths that occur on many conifers, often brought about by a mechanical or viral shock, and can usually be seen in the upper branches of trees, looking a bit like a bird's nest at first glance.

The shape of a tree can change as it matures. The upper branches of many conifers may take on a more horizontal appearance after a certain age. Thus the cedar of Lebanon will be broadly pyramidal in shape in its early years, but will take its more familiar spreading form after it reaches about 12m/40ft. In many conifers, the branches, although starting in a more upright position, will eventually sag well past the horizontal and take on the drooping habit that is one of the family's attractions. In some cases the droop becomes excessive and the branches hang down limply against the trunk, as in *Sequoiadendron giganteum*, 'Pendulum'. Conversely, in some forms the branches tend to grow upright, forming columnar – or fastigiate – trees.

The growth rate of conifers varies considerably. Some start slowly, then suddenly

LEFT AND BELOW: *Most conifers form very large trees in the wild, but in cultivation there is a wide variety of shapes and sizes.*

put on a spurt, much to the dismay of those who planted them in the rock garden, expecting them to stay dwarf. Others rise rapidly to, say, 12 or 18m/40 to 60ft and then slow down. Environmental factors may influence the growth rate. Exposure to winds, for example, will slow down the rate, as will being planted in a poor or dry soil. It is difficult to influence the rate of growth of some families. In pines, for example, the forthcoming buds have all been laid down the previous year, so that fertilizer will not immediately stimulate new growth.

Most of the species that will tolerate clipping to form a hedge can also be used to form topiary, but slow-growing plants, such as yew, are best as they hold their shape better and require less attention.

RIGHT: *There is a good choice of conifers for containers and even alpine beds.*

GARDEN USES

Conifers vary considerably in size and shape, making them suitable for growing in any size of garden, even gardens in containers or on balconies. There is also a wide range of colours. The variety of evergreen plants allows the gardener to give structure and colour to the garden throughout the year. Another advantage is that they are virtually maintenance-free, thus involving little work or cost.

The prime use of conifers is as specimen trees or as part of a group. For specimens, shape is very important, especially if they are silhouetted. They make admirable focal points in the garden.

One of the major uses is as hedging and windbreaks. A large number of species is suitable for this work. However it is important to take into consideration growth rates and final heights. Yew is slow-growing, and while it will take some time to make a thick hedge it will not need clipping more than once a year. On the other hand, Leyland cypress will very quickly produce a substantial hedge, but it will not stop growing and will need to be constantly trimmed.

LEFT AND BELOW:
In larger plantings, individual conifers should be chosen to complement each other in colour and form.

L E F T : A few conifers have blue, or grayish green foliage.

R I G H T : There is a wide spectrum of colours in the foliage of conifers.

R I G H T :
Towering cypresses are seen at their best in parkland plantings.

SOIL CONDITIONS

In the wild, conifers often live in regions that either have a poor, dry soil, or that have periods of drought, especially in summer. Generally, therefore, they will tolerate free-draining conditions and poor soils. However, like most trees, they do best when they have had plenty of well-rotted organic material added to the soil. This not only provides a slow release of nutrients but also helps to retain moisture. A few conifers need these conditions or they begin to lose their leaves and become rather scruffy. On the whole, most conifers do not like to grow in wet or water-logged soil. Unless you are hoping to grow swamp cypresses or one of the other moisture loving species, it is important to install some form of drainage.

PLANTING

Set out young conifers at any time between autumn and spring, whenever the weather and soil are suitable. Container-grown plants can be planted out at other times, but it is essential that the young trees do not dry out. Remove all perennial weeds from the soil and incorporate some well-rotted humus around the planting hole. If the plant has become pot-bound (the roots are wound round in a tight tangle), gently tease them out. Set the plant into the hole at the same level as it was in its container or nursery bed.

Taller plants that are liable to suffer from wind rock will need staking. The stake can be positioned before the conifer is planted, so that the roots are not damaged by its insertion. Tie the trunk low down, so that it keeps the base of the plant steady but allows the top to move freely. If the base moves, so will the root-ball, severing any new roots that are trying to move out into the surrounding soil.

Fill the hole with soil and gently but firmly press it down around the roots. Water the planting hole and the area immediately adjacent.

PRUNING

Specimen trees rarely need pruning other than to remove any dead or damaged branches and to occasionally remove a rogue branch that has strayed out of position. Occasionally a young tree will be damaged and two instead of one leaders may develop. It may be necessary to remove one of these if you want a regular tree. Some trees will need to be cut back to keep them within bounds, while others, such as hedges and topiary, will need constant attention.

When removing branches or a false leader, cut flush to the trunk without damaging the bark. There is no need to dress the wounds. Genera like the yews can be cut back into old wood and they will produce more buds and regenerate, but others, such as *Cupressus macrocarpa*, are reluctant to shoot from old wood, and pruning should be restricted to trimming back the current year's growth.

AFTERCARE

A tree planted in summer will need constant watering through the first year to allow the roots to establish. A thorough watering, not just a surface damping, is essential. With a winter planting the tree should be able to look after itself during the hotter months, but should be watered during prolonged periods without rain. A mulch will help preserve moisture.

A mulch will also help to keep down the weeds. It is essential that weeds are not allowed to clamber up through the young branches, preventing light reaching the leaves and using up vital moisture and nutrients. Weed, either by hand or, if you must, with a chemical control.

Wind can cause a lot of damage to young trees, especially those that have not yet established roots. Windbreak netting

GLOSSARY

ADPRESSED: pressed against the stem.

ARIL: a sticky cover to certain seeds, such as in the yew.

COIR: a substitute for peat made from coconut fibre.

COLUMNAR: shaped like a column.

CULTIVAR: a particular named form of a species raised in cultivation.

DECIDUOUS: sheds its leaves in the autumn.

DIOECIOUS: of a species where male and female flowers are carried on separate plants.

EVERGREEN: holds on to its leaves throughout the year.

FASTIGIATE: of a plant in which the branches are held upward against the trunk, forming a column.

GENUS: a group of plants linked together by botanical similarities.

GLABROUS: without hairs.

GLAUCOUS: of leaves that have a waxy bluish bloom on them.

GLOBOSE: roughly spherical in shape.

LEADER: the main growing shoot at the top of the stem of a tree.

PENDULOUS: weeping.

PROSTRATE: lying on the ground.

PYRAMIDAL: having tapering sides and ending in a point.

REFLEXED: curved outward or back on itself.

SESSILE: without a stalk.

SPECIES: individual plants that make up a genus.

SPORT: a plant derived from a branch or shoot that is a mutant of the parent plant.

SPREADING: growing sideways rather than upward. Often irregular in shape.

placed to one side or all around the plants will help prevent dessication and other damage.

Damage can also be caused by mammals. If the garden cannot be wired off as a whole, individual trees will need to be protected. This can be achieved by placing wire-netting around them, or by using a plastic sleeve that slips round the trunk.

Keep an eye on any tree ties. Slacken them a bit if they appear to be biting into the bark as the trunk expands.

HARDINESS ZONES

Each entry in The Conifer Identifier ends with a zone number, identifying the temperature zone in which the conifer is hardy.

°F	Zone	°C
below −50	1	below −45
−50 to −40	2	−45 to −40
−40 to −30	3	−40 to −34
−30 to −20	4	−34 to −29
−20 to −10	5	−29 to −23
−10 to 0	6	−23 to −17
0 to 10	7	−17 to −12
10 to 20	8	−12 to −7
20 to 30	9	−7 to −1
30 to 40	10	−1 to 5

THE CONIFER IDENTIFIER

The Conifer Identifier is the body of the book. It identifies 99 conifers in 21 genera, in entries arranged in alphabetical order, first of genera, then of species and cultivars. Each genus has a brief introduction, then each of the conifers within it is identified by a photograph, its family, genus, and common names, and a short description of its distinguishing characteristics. The entries also give an estimate of growth in the first ten years, cultivation needs for each conifer, and a guide to garden situation. Below is a key to symbols used in the entries. They provide a visual key to size, shape, colour, and other characteristics that are useful to know for garden planning and design.

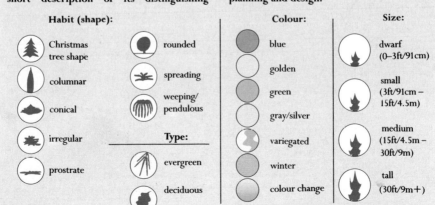

Habit (shape):
- Christmas tree shape
- columnar
- conical
- irregular
- prostrate
- rounded
- spreading
- weeping/pendulous

Type:
- evergreen
- deciduous

Colour:
- blue
- golden
- green
- gray/silver
- variegated
- winter
- colour change

Size:
- dwarf (0–3ft/91cm)
- small (3ft/91cm – 15ft/4.5m)
- medium (15ft/4.5m – 30ft/9m)
- tall (30ft/9m+)

ABIES (PINACEAE)
SILVER FIRS

There are 55 species of Silver fir, making them the second largest genus in the Pine family. They are found throughout the northern hemisphere in both cold and mild areas. Apart from some Mexican species, the majority are hardy in most areas. Not all species are worthy of cultivation, but allowing for cultivars, there are about 100 different plants in gardens around the world.

The majority are upright trees of medium to tall stature, while a few are much lower and bushy. They are mainly regular in shape. The flattish, needlelike leaves are smooth and leathery. They are attached to the branch by a circular, sucker-like pad which leaves a scar when removed. They are arranged all round the shoot, but tend to flop to one side or the other so that they form a "parting", growing in two lines on either side of the branch. They are mainly green above with silver bands on the reverse. The cones are either cylindrical or barrel-shaped and are held erect. They vary in colour from brown to green and purplish-blue, and often have secretions of white resin on them. They are difficult to collect for use indoors as they break up and shed their seed on the tree.

ABIES BALSAMEA 'HUDSONIA'
HUDSON'S BALSAM FIR

Many so-called rock garden conifers soon outgrow their positions, but *Abies balsamea* 'Hudsonia' is truly dwarf. Its compact shape means that it can be used as sentinels to a path or set of steps, but its best use is on a rock garden, where it helps to give a natural feel to the miniature landscape.

ORIGIN The balsam fir comes from Canada. 'Hudsonia' is a garden form.

MATURE HEIGHT 75cm/30in (10 years – 30cm/12in).

SHAPE Generally a rounded shape, although slightly wider than tall.

LEAVES Dark green with a white tip. They are arranged in two rows on either side of the stem. They smell of balsam when crushed.

CULTIVATION No special attention is required other than patience, as this tree is very slow-growing.

SITUATION Rock gardens and scree beds.

HARDINESS Zone 3.

ABIES KOREANA
KOREAN FIR

Although not seen frequently in the wild, this has become a very popular garden plant. This is mainly because of its attractive blue cones, but it also has a very even shape and beautiful foliage. If there is only space for one of the taller conifers, this may well be the one to choose. There is a dwarf form available.

ORIGIN Korea.

MATURE HEIGHT 10m/30ft (10 years – 3m/10ft).

SHAPE This tree has a classic Christmas tree shape.

LEAVES Dark green with a glaucous blue backing; the new spring growth is silvery gray.

CULTIVATION No problems in cultivation, although this tree can be damaged by wind.

SITUATION Small to medium-sized gardens.

HARDINESS Zone 5.

ABIES LASIOCARPA 'COMPACTA'
DWARF ARIZONA FIR

The species is a tall-growing tree, but this variety, as its name implies, is a neat, compact form. It has a classic fir-tree shape and its delightful silvery colour makes it an ideal plant for the small garden or for a large rock garden. It will contrast well with green foliage conifers and so will be suitable for a mixed bed of conifers.

ORIGIN The species comes from Arizona, USA, but the form 'Compacta' is of garden origin.

MATURE HEIGHT 5m/15ft (10 years – 75cm/30in).

SHAPE Almost forms a classic Christmas tree shape, but the bottom branches are shorter, making it slightly ovoid.

LEAVES A beautiful silvery blue.

CULTIVATION This tree is slow growing, so it can be used in a rock garden, but it will eventually outgrow its position and need replacing.

SITUATION Small to medium sized gardens. Large rock gardens.

HARDINESS Zone 5.

ARAUCARIA (ARAUCARIACEAE)
MONKEY PUZZLES

It may come as a surprise to learn that there are, in fact (depending which botanist you follow), 14–18 different species of monkey puzzle, because only one is generally known in cultivation. They all come from the southern hemisphere, from Australasia and South America.

The monkey puzzles are characterized by long, sweeping branches covered with overlapping, scale-like leaves. They are dioecious, that is to say, male and female flowers are born on different trees, so that you will require at least one of each sex to get any seed. The cones are large and globular.

The trees are generally rather tall and are really only suitable for larger gardens. One of the smallest is the smooth Tasmanian cedar, *Araucaria cupressoides*, but this is only hardy to Zone 8.

ARAUCARIA ARAUCANA
MONKEY PUZZLE

For those who have space, this is a wonderfully attractive tree. The puzzle is created by the difficulty in collecting the cones with their edible seed when the leaves are so very prickly. A well-grown specimen has branches sweeping to the ground; those that have been planted too close together usually only have branches at the top, and a long, bare trunk beneath.

ORIGIN Chile and Argentina.

MATURE HEIGHT 24m/80ft (10 years – 6m/20ft).

SHAPE A well-clothed tree is conical.

LEAVES The branches are clothed in bright green leather plates that are extremely prickly.

CULTIVATION Prefers a moist humusy soil to a dry one. Fast-growing
to start with, then slows down. Propagate from seed only.

SITUATION Large gardens and parks.

HARDINESS Zone 7.

CALOCEDRUS (CUPRESSACEAE)
INCENSE CEDARS

The incense cedars form a small genus of three species, of which *Calocedrus decurrens*, from North America, is the only one in general cultivation. *C. macrolepsis*, from Hunan in China, and *C. formosana*, from Taiwan, are just about in cultivation, but are rarely seen. *C. decurrens* is a tall tree, while the other two have a much shorter stature. However, they are all rather too large for the average garden, only being really suitable for larger spaces. The leaves are scale-like and are carried in two rows down either side of the shoot. They appear in typical fan-like sprays. The cones are vase-shaped and leathery. Unfortunately, they are small and rather insignificant.

CALOCEDRUS DECURRENS
INCENSE CEDAR

The incense cedar is an attractive tree, rounded when young, but becoming increasingly columnar with age. Upright leathery cones can be seen in profusion in some years on older plants. Cedar is the main wood used in the manufacture of pencils. There is a variegated form, 'Aureovariegata', and a golden-leaved variety, 'Berrima Gold'.
ORIGIN Pacific coast of North America.
MATURE HEIGHT 24m/80ft (10 years – 4.5m/15ft).
SHAPE Columnar.
LEAVES Deep green, slightly paler beneath. Carried in flat fans.
CULTIVATION Immune to honey fungus. Tends to defoliate on thin or dry soils.
SITUATION Medium to large gardens.
HARDINESS Zone 5.

CEDRUS (PINACEAE)
CEDARS

There are only four species of cedar: *Cedrus atlantica*, *C. brevifolia*, *C. deodara*, and *C. libani*, and the first two are sometimes classed as varieties of *C. libani*. There are plenty of cultivars for the garden, varying in height from mature trees as tall as 60m/200ft to those that are ground-hugging. They come from around the Mediterranean and from the western Himalayas. They are all hardy. The wild species tend to be slender pyramidal in shape while they are still relatively young, but as they mature the tops begin to spread, eventually making the flat-topped specimens that one associates with the huge cedar of Lebanon. The garden forms exhibit a wide range of shapes, including those that are completely prostrate. The leaves are needlelike and are gathered in whorls, although on new shoots they are generally arranged in spirals. They tend to be bluish green or green, but cultivars exhibit a range of foliage colour. The cones are distinctively barrel-shaped and are carried erect on the branches. The species make good plants for larger gardens and parkland.

CEDRUS ATLANTICA 'GLAUCA PENDULA'
WEEPING BLUE CEDAR

The Atlas cedar has several interesting forms, of which the weeping blue cedar is the most beautiful. Unlike its parent, this is not an upright tree but a spreading one with weeping branches. A mature tree has much the look of a frozen waterfall about it, with branches cascading to the ground. It is very slow-growing.

ORIGIN Of garden origin.
MATURE HEIGHT Height of the original graft.
SHAPE Main branches spread, from which subsidiary branches weep.
LEAVES Short needles of a delicate blue colour.
CULTIVATION The height of the tree depends on the height of the initial graft.
SITUATION Any size of garden.
HARDINESS Zone 6.

CEDRUS DEODARA
DEODAR

This plant is a very graceful tree, with pendulous, almost weeping branches. It is particularly attractive when young. The cones are barrel-shaped and attractive. There are several good forms, including 'Argentea' and 'Aurea', which have silver and golden foliage respectively. Others are described below.

ORIGIN Western Himalayas.
MATURE HEIGHT 24m/80ft (10 years – 5m/16ft).
SHAPE Pyramidal with long, weeping branches.
LEAVES Blue-green when young, dark green in older trees.
CULTIVATION A warm, maritime atmosphere produces a more pendulous plant. However it will tolerate a dry position.
SITUATION Small to large gardens.
HARDINESS Zone 7.

CEDRUS DEODARA 'GOLDEN HORIZON'
GOLDEN HORIZON DEODAR

It is difficult to imagine that this is the same species as the deodar. It is a low-growing, semi-prostrate plant that is perfect for cascading down a bank or spreading over the ground. Its pendulous branches give it a rather untidy appearance, but at the same time often create an exciting shape. It is widely available.

ORIGIN Garden origin.
MATURE HEIGHT 1.5m/5ft (10 years – 60cm/2ft).
SHAPE Semi-prostrate and loosely spreading.
LEAVES Short needles. Golden green, but much bluer if grown in shade.
CULTIVATION Will grow in quite dry conditions, including on old walls.
SITUATION Small to medium-sized gardens.
HARDINESS Zone 7.

C*EDRUS LIBANI*
CEDAR OF LEBANON

The huge horizontal limbs of this tree give a sense of tranquillity to a garden or park. It has been known since biblical times. The biggest specimens are several hundreds of years old, but the tree grows with surprising rapidity in its early years – about 15cm/1ft per year for 70 years – and then slows down. The cones are barrel-shaped.

ORIGIN Lebanon, Syria, Turkey.

MATURE HEIGHT 40m/130ft (10 years – 6m/20ft).

SHAPE Young trees are slender pyramids, but they become flat-topped as they mature.

LEAVES Dark green, densely packed, and carried in horizontal tiers giving the tree its characteristic appearance.

CULTIVATION No special attention is required. The long branches may be snapped by excessive snowfalls.

SITUATION Parkland or large gardens.

HARDINESS Zone 5.

C*EDRUS LIBANI* '*PENDULA*'
WEEPING CEDAR OF LEBANON

Most people are so familiar with the majestic cedar of Lebanon that they do not realize that there are small tree forms that can be grown in any size of garden. 'Pendula' makes an absolutely splendid weeping tree, you can almost see the tears cascading down. 'Sargentii' is another weeping form, but it is usually grown as a prostrate plant.

ORIGIN Of garden origin.

MATURE HEIGHT 6m/20ft (10 years – 1.5m/5ft).

SHAPE Decidedly pendulous.

LEAVES Mid-green; fresh growth is a very pale green.

CULTIVATION No problems.

SITUATION Any size of garden.

HARDINESS Zone 6.

CHAMAECYPARIS (CUPRESSACEAE)
FALSE CYPRESSES

The false cypresses consist of six wild species and innumerable cultivars suitable for any size of garden. They originate on both coasts of North America, and in Japan and Taiwan. Apart from the Taiwan species *(Chamaecyparis formosensis)* all are hardy. In the wild, the species make tall trees, up to 60m/200ft, often spreading in shape. Garden varieties vary from dwarf rock-garden plants to tall specimens. The shape in cultivation is narrow and columnar, although a few are more widely pyramidal. The false cypresses differ from the true cypresses in that the leaves have a flattened profile. The branches are also flat and fan-like, as opposed to being more three-dimensional. The two have been crossed to produce the popular Leyland cypress, x *Cupressocyparis leylandii*. The variation in shape, size, texture, and colour of the garden cultivars make this a very favoured genus. Undoubtedly the most popular is the Lawson cypress, *C. lawsoniana*, which has given rise to well over 200 cultivars. The foliage colour of the species is generally green, but in cultivation there is now a tremendous range of colour.

CHAMAECYPARIS LAWSONIANA 'CHILWORTH SILVER'
CHILWORTH SILVER LAWSONIANA

The main attraction of this plant is its juvenile foliage, which is a delightful silvery blue. As it ages, it turns greener, but still retains its basic blue colour. The shrub is slow-growing, producing a neat, broadly columnar shape with tight upright branches. It is a sport from *C.l.* 'Ellwoodii'.

ORIGIN Of garden origin in Great Britain.
MATURE HEIGHT 2m/7ft (10 years – 90cm/3ft).
SHAPE Broadly columnar.
LEAVES Silvery blue when young.
CULTIVATION No problems in cultivation.
SITUATION Any size of garden.
HARDINESS Zone 6.

CHAMAECYPARIS LAWSONIANA 'COLUMNARIS'
COLUMNAR LAWSONIANA

As well as having a very elegant shape, this is one of the best blue-leaved forms of this species. The very narrow columnar shape makes this form of the Lawsoniana ideal for planting as an accent plant. It is so narrow and slow-growing that, in spite of its ultimate height, it can be used in a small garden.

ORIGIN Of garden origin in the Netherlands.
MATURE HEIGHT 10m/30ft (10 years – 2.5m/8ft).
SHAPE Columnar.
LEAVES Upward-facing blue sprays.
CULTIVATION No problems in cultivation.
SITUATION Any size of garden.
HARDINESS Zone 6.

CHAMAECYPARIS LAWSONIANA 'DOW'S GEM'
DOW'S GEM LAWSONIANA

Dow's Gem is a wonderful form of Lawsoniana. It is a spreading variety, but as it puts on growth, the shape becomes more spherical. However, it does not lose its general loose shaggy appearance, which makes it most attractive. It is also known as 'Dow's Variety'.

ORIGIN Of garden origin in the USA.
MATURE HEIGHT 3m/10ft (10 years – 90cm/3ft).
SHAPE Spreading, becoming spherical.
LEAVES Coarse bluish-green foliage with a white bloom on the underside, slightly drooping.
CULTIVATION It can be pruned to keep a more regular shape.
SITUATION Medium to large gardens.
HARDINESS Zone 6.

CHAMAECYPARIS LAWSONIANA 'ELLWOOD'S GOLD'
ELLWOOD'S GOLDEN LAWSONIANA

This is one of the most popular golden-foliaged conifers. It was found as a sport from 'Ellwoodii', the parent of all the group that bears its name. In this form the green foliage is gold-tipped. The gold is more noticeable in spring and early summer; toward autumn it begins to look green. It is quite slow-growing.

ORIGIN Of garden origin from a western North American tree.
MATURE HEIGHT 4.5m/15ft (10 years – 1.5m/5ft).
SHAPE Columnar.
LEAVES Flat sprays, yellow- or golden-tipped in spring and early summer.
CULTIVATION Although often recommended as a rock garden plant, this tree will eventually grow too large.
SITUATION Small to medium gardens.
HARDINESS Zone 6.

CHAMAECYPARIS LAWSONIANA 'FILIFORMIS COMPACTA'
COMPACT FILAMENTOUS LAWSONIANA

The 'Filiformis' Lawsonianas have a very different distinct foliage form. They are much more linear, with the narrow sprays of leaves limply hanging as threads from the tips of the branches, giving the impression that the whole bush is dripping. This form has a conical shape and is less wayward than some of the others. It is very slow-growing.

ORIGIN Of garden origin.
MATURE HEIGHT 1.5m/5ft (10 years – 75cm/30in).
SHAPE Conical.
LEAVES Threadlike, bluish green.
CULTIVATION No cultivation problems.
SITUATION Any size of garden, including large rock gardens.
HARDINESS Zone 5.

CHAMAECYPARIS LAWSONIANA 'FLETCHERI'

FLETCHER'S LAWSON CYPRESS

This is an extremely popular tree. 'Fletcheri' is variable, with some forms much looser than others. The permanently semi-juvenile foliage is an attractive blue-green. This tree will eventually become rather tall, but it can still be grown in a small garden if you are prepared to replace it.

ORIGIN Of garden origin.

MATURE HEIGHT 6m/20ft (10 years – 2.5m/8ft).

SHAPE Pyramidal, eventually becoming columnar.

LEAVES Blue-green.

CULTIVATION Does best in cooler climates. Slow-growing at first, but beware, it suddenly becomes a rapid grower.

SITUATION Any size of garden.

HARDINESS Zone 6.

CHAMAECYPARIS LAWSONIANA 'GIMBORNII'

GIMBORN'S LAWSONIANA

'Gimbornii' is a very dense, spherical plant with both its branches and foliage very tightly packed. It has the advantage of being very slow-growing, and never gets very big, making a good shrub for a small garden. Its distinctive shape means that it can be used as a feature in the garden.

ORIGIN Of garden origin in the Netherlands.

MATURE HEIGHT 1.8m/6ft (10 years – 75cm/30in).

SHAPE Spherical.

LEAVES Dark green, tinged with blue.

CULTIVATION Should need no pruning to keep its shape, but any outgrowths should be removed to prevent distortion of the shape.

SITUATION Any size of garden. Will suit large rock gardens.

HARDINESS Zone 6.

CHAMAECYPARIS LAWSONIANA 'GREEN PILLAR'
GREEN PILLAR LAWSONIANA

It is the fresh green colour of the foliage of this plant, plus its pleasing columnar shape, that makes it so attractive. During the spring the leaves also have a hint of gold about them, which brightens their appearance even more. The shape is not so rigid as some, but this adds to its character.

ORIGIN Of garden origin in Great Britain.
MATURE HEIGHT 6m/20ft (10 years – 3m/10ft).
SHAPE Columnar.
LEAVES A fresh green, tinged with gold in spring.
CULTIVATION No problems in cultivation.
SITUATION Medium to large gardens.
HARDINESS Zone 6.

CHAMAECYPARIS LAWSONIANA 'HILLIERI'
HILLIER'S LAWSONIANA

'Hillieri' is one of the best golden Lawsonianas. It has a very graceful, pyramidal shape and slightly drooping foliage. This variety is a bright golden colour in the spring, but turns greener as the seasons progress. Although it eventually becomes rather tall, it is very slow-growing and can be grown in a small garden.

ORIGIN Of garden origin in Great Britain.
MATURE HEIGHT 10m/30ft (10 years 2m/7ft).
SHAPE Narrow pyramid.
LEAVES Golden yellow.
CULTIVATION Protect from cold winds or the golden foliage burns.
SITUATION Any size of garden.
HARDINESS Zone 6.

CHAMAECYPARIS LAWSONIANA 'PEMBURY BLUE'
PEMBURY BLUE

This is undoubtedly the best of all blue-leaved Lawsonianas. It forms a narrow pyramidal tree with loose, pendulous branches. Unfortunately, it will grow too large for the small garden, but could be replaced after ten years. It is hardier than many of the other cultivars.

ORIGIN Of garden origin in Great Britain.
MATURE HEIGHT 10m/30ft (10 years – 4m/13ft).
SHAPE Narrowly pyramidal, becoming broadly columnar.
LEAVES Sprays of slatey blue.
CULTIVATION No cultivation.
SITUATION Medium to large gardens.
HARDINESS Zone 5.

CHAMAECYPARIS LAWSONIANA 'TAMARISCIFOLIA'
TAMARISK-LEAVED LAWSONIANA

This is an attractive, rounded form of Lawsoniana in which the sprays of leaves are layered, almost like waves reaching a shore. In the majority of gardens it only reaches about 2m/7ft but there are some very old specimens that are almost double that. It does not have a single trunk but a collection of main stems.

ORIGIN Of garden origin in Great Britain.
MATURE HEIGHT 2m/7ft (10 years – 75cm/30in).
SHAPE Flat-topped, open bush.
LEAVES Mid-green.
CULTIVATION No problems in cultivation.
SITUATION Although ultimately quite large, it is slow-growing enough for small gardens.
HARDINESS Zone 5.

CHAMAECYPARIS NOOTKATENSIS
NOOTKA CYPRESS

These are not trees for the small garden, they rapidly grow into forest giants. They form vast pyramids of perfect shape, clad in a close foliage, under which nothing else can grow. They make wonderful specimen trees if there is the space. There are several cultivars including 'Compacta', which only reaches 2m/7ft.

ORIGIN Western North America.
MATURE HEIGHT 30m/100ft (10 years – 7.5m/25ft).
SHAPE Tall pyramids.
LEAVES Dark gray-green, although there are golden and variegated cultivars.
CULTIVATION No problems in cultivation except for its size if this is not anticipated.
SITUATION Large gardens and parkland.
HARDINESS Zone 4.

CHAMAECYPARIS OBTUSA 'KOSTERI'
KOSTER'S HINOKI CYPRESS

This is a wonderfully decorative plant, with each horizontal fan of leaves undulating from side to side, each building up in layers or tiers to create a piece of modern sculpture. It should be given a place of prominence, so that the shape of the small tree and its leaves can be appreciated.

ORIGIN Of garden origin in the Netherlands.
MATURE HEIGHT 1.2m/4ft (10 years – 75cm/30in).
SHAPE An irregular pyramid.
LEAVES Bright mid-green in an undulating fan.
CULTIVATION It can be sprawling, but a more upright plant can be had by training the leader against a stake.
SITUATION Any size of garden. Can be grown on large rock gardens.
HARDINESS Zone 5.

CHAMAECYPARIS OBTUSA 'NANA LUTEA'
DWARF YELLOW HINOKI CYPRESS

As its name suggests, this is a yellow-leaved form of this fascinating shrub. As with 'Kosteri', the leaves are wavy fans arranged in tiers like a wedding cake. This creates a wonderful sense of rhythm in the plant, even when the wind is not blowing. It is very slow-growing and can be used on the rock garden, without outgrowing its position.

ORIGIN Of garden origin.

MATURE HEIGHT 2m/7ft (10 years – 50cm/20in).

SHAPE An irregular pyramid.

LEAVES Fan-shaped sprays in golden yellow, but greenish yellow on the underside and in the shade.

CULTIVATION Avoid planting in the shade or the foliage loses its golden intensity.

SITUATION Any size of garden. Good for the rock garden.

HARDINESS Zone 5.

CHAMAECYPARIS PISIFERA 'COMPACTA'
COMPACT SAWARA CYPRESS

This is a pleasant plant, but not spectacular. It forms a tight, conical hummock and, being very slow-growing, is ideally suited to the rock garden. The foliage is a bluish-green, a brighter green in spring, and browner in winter. The flattish sprays of leaves droop slightly, giving an interesting texture to the plant.

ORIGIN Of garden origin.

MATURE HEIGHT 45cm/18in (10 years – 23cm/8in).

SHAPE Flattish cone.

LEAVES Bluish green; browner in winter.

CULTIVATION Remove any stronger growths that spoil the shape.

SITUATION Any size of garden. It also does well on any size of rock garden.

HARDINESS Zone 5.

CHAMAECYPARIS PISIFERA 'GOLDEN MOP'
GOLDEN MOP SAWARA CYPRESS

This low plant is well named as it looks like a slightly wayward mop of golden hair. It does not grow into a very big plant, but flops effectively over the ground, making it ideal for the rock garden. The foliage is similar to many of the Filifera cultivars, with pendulous, wiry tips to the shoots. It is bright gold.
ORIGIN Of garden origin.
MATURE HEIGHT 45cm/18in (10 years   30cm/12in).
SHAPE Prostrate.
LEAVES Long shoots of adpressed leaves, golden green in colour.
CULTIVATION Do not plant in shade or the leaves will become greener. It does not burn in bright sun, a problem with many golden-leaved plants.
SITUATION Any size of garden.
HARDINESS Zone 5.

CHAMAECYPARIS PISIFERA 'SUNGOLD'
SUNGOLD SAWARA CYPRESS

This wonderful shrub has graceful arching stems, the tips of which seem to drip with greenish yellow leaves. The colour varies, depending on the climate. It is golden green in cooler areas and golden brown in hotter parts of the world. It is sometimes known, incorrectly, as *C.p.* 'Filifera Sungold' and bears a great resemblance to the other 'Filifera' cultivars.
ORIGIN Of garden origin in the Netherlands.
MATURE HEIGHT 3m/10ft (10 years – 90cm/3ft).
SHAPE Conical.
LEAVES Long shoots of adpress leaves, golden green in colour.
CULTIVATION Do not plant in shade or the leaves will become greener. It does not burn in bright sun, a problem with many golden-leaved plants.
SITUATION Any size of garden.
HARDINESS Zone 5.

CRYPTOMERIA (TAXODIACEAE)
JAPANESE CEDARS

This is a small genus of two species: *C. japonica* from Japan and *C. fortunei* from southern China. Some botanists have classified the latter as a variety of *C. japonica*, namely *C.j. sinensis*, thus reducing the genus to a single species. The Japanese cedars are closely related to the *Sequoiadendron* and are separated from it by only minor botanical differences. They are very distinct conifers, with leaves that are more like awls than needles, tapering along their length.

Japanese cedars have been in cultivation for a long time, during which many cultivars have arisen. Although some are large, many of these cultivars are quite small and make ideal plants for the smaller garden. They make good specimen trees or can be used with other shrubs. The large varieties often form huge spreading bushes that are hollow in the middle, to the delight of children.

CRYPTOMERIA JAPONICA 'ELEGANS'
ELEGANS JAPANESE CEDAR

The wonderful thing about this tree is that it retains its soft, hazy, juvenile foliage. This is a bluish green in summer, but turns a superb reddish bronze in winter. On mature trees the foliage can look like billowing clouds. The trees can become very tall and sometimes grow at an angle, or with multiple stems, forming a bizarre-looking plant.
ORIGIN China.
MATURE HEIGHT 12m/40ft (10 years – 3m/10ft).
SHAPE Varies, but is broadly columnar or conical when erect, spreading when it has several main stems.
LEAVES Soft juvenile foliage.
CULTIVATION No problems in cultivation.
SITUATION Large gardens and parkland.
HARDINESS Zone 6.

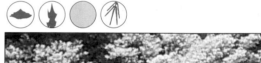

CRYPTOMERIA JAPONICA 'ELEGANS COMPACTA'
COMPACT ELEGANS JAPANESE CEDAR

While *Cryptomeria japonica* is too big for anything but a large garden, this form should fit into any size of garden, although it still has quite a bit of vigour. It has the same beautiful, billowing foliage as 'Elegans', but in a more contained plant. It is roughly conical in shape.
ORIGIN Of garden origin.
MATURE HEIGHT 3m/10ft (10 years – 1.8m/6ft).
SHAPE Conical or rounded.
LEAVES Fine juvenile leaves, bluish green in summer, reddish bronze in winter.
CULTIVATION No problems in cultivation.
SITUATION Any size of garden, although it may outgrow small ones.
HARDINESS Zone 5.

x *CUPRESSOCYPARIS (CUPRESSACEAE)*
LEYLAND CYPRESSES

A series of hybrids between *Chamaecyparis nootkatensis* and various species of *Cupressus* – *C. macrocarpa* in the case of the only common form, x *C. leylandii* (the "x" indicates that it is a cross between two different genera). Other forms are in existence but rarely seen. All the hybrids are sterile, so all plants need to be raised from cuttings. The original crosses occurred accidentally in 1888, and again in 1911, from whence all plants have come. They exhibit all the vigour of a first cross, growing fast and, unless pruned, making tall trees. There are several cultivars, including different coloured foliage forms, all raised from sports.
The leaves are scale-like, tightly pressed to the shoots, which are arranged in a flat spray. They are mainly dark green but there are cultivars of various greens, blues, and gold. There are also several variegated forms.

x *CUPRESSOCYPARIS LEYLANDII*
LEYLAND CYPRESS

The most popular of the *Chamaecyparis* – *Cupressus* crosses, the Leyland cypress is extremely fast-growing, capable of putting on 90cm/3ft a year for the first 20 years or so. It is tough, being both hardy and disease-resistant. Its impressive stature makes it an ideal specimen plant, but its toughness and speed of growth also make it a very good hedging plant.

ORIGIN Of garden origin in Great Britain.
MATURE HEIGHT 30m/100ft (10 years – 7.5m/25ft).
SHAPE Columnar.
LEAVES Dark green, but also golden and blue cultivars.
CULTIVATION Will grow on most soils, including wet ones. If grown as a hedge, it needs constant clipping.
SITUATION Medium to large gardens. Suitable for small gardens only if pruned.
HARDINESS Zone 4.

CUPRESSUS (CUPRESSACEAE)
CYPRESSES

There are about 20 different species and a large number of cultivars of *Cupressus*. They are very closely related to the false cypresses, *Chamaecyparis*, and are often difficult to tell apart. The main obvious difference is that in many of the cypresses, the sprays of scale-like leaves are more three-dimensional, as opposed to the flat ones of the false cypresses. The cones are spherical and are made up of very hard scales, a bit like the sections of a soccer ball. One of the best known trees of this genus is the columnar Italian cypress, *C. sempervirens*, so distinctive of Mediterranean gardens and hillsides, but it is not reliably hardy (minimum of Zone 7).

These trees are valuable, as they happily grow in dry, hot conditions, even in poor soils. They should not be planted in the shade. Their shape means that they are often used as specimen trees or as a focal point.

CUPRESSUS GLABRA
SMOOTH ARIZONA CYPRESS

A delightful small tree with a good blue foliage that seems to go every which-way, like a tangle of barbed wire, except that it is not prickly. This tree was originally known as *C. arizonica glabra,* under which name it is still sometimes sold, but it has a smooth flaking bark unlike the more stringy texture of *C. arizonica.*

ORIGIN Arizona, USA.
MATURE HEIGHT 15m/50ft (10 years – 4m/13ft).
SHAPE Pyramidal.
LEAVES Narrow in short spray and bluish gray in colour, flecked with white resin.
CULTIVATION Does well on dry soils.
SITUATION Medium to large gardens.
HARDINESS Zone 6.

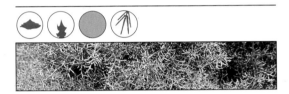

CUPRESSUS MACROCARPA 'DONARD GOLD'
DONARD'S GOLD MONTEREY CYPRESS

'Donard Gold' is a very fine form of the Macrocarpa. It forms a small pyramidal or columnar tree, with a bright golden foliage held in upright sprays. It makes a good specimen plant or part of a mixed planting. In milder areas it could be used as a golden hedge, and its foliage is good in flower arrangements.

ORIGIN Northern Ireland.
MATURE HEIGHT 30m/100ft (10 years – 4m/13ft).
SHAPE Conical or broadly columnar.
LEAVES Golden.
CULTIVATION No problems in cultivation.
SITUATION Medium to large gardens.
HARDINESS Zone 7.

GINKGO (GINKGOACEAE)
GINKGO, MAIDENHAIR TREE

This is an extraordinary tree that at first sight does not look like a conifer at all. It is a very ancient genus, known from fossils found all over the world, but now restricted to one genus found in two remote areas of southern China. In many ways it has a close relationship to another ancient group of plants, the tree ferns. Not only do the leaves have similarities, but the method of pollination is the same. This tree's alternative name relates to the similarity of its foliage to that of a maidenhair fern.
Ginkgo are extremely hardy. They are best used as specimen plants, rather than lost in a group of other trees, being particularly excellent for planting on lawns. Although there is only one species, there are several cultivars exhibiting different shapes and leaf colours.

GINKGO TRILOBA
GINKGO, MAIDENHAIR TREE

This is an intriguing tree to grow. It has deciduous leaves in the form of flat paddles, a bit like ducks' feet. They are borne in groups of three on long stalks. They are light green in spring and summer, but a wonderful golden colour in autumn. The male forms are preferred to the females, as the latter produce a foetid-smelling fruit.

ORIGIN Southern China.
MATURE HEIGHT 30m/100ft (10 years – 6m/20ft).
SHAPE Similar to that of most conventional deciduous trees.
LEAVES Flat, paddle-shaped, more deeply divided into three lobes in younger plants.
CULTIVATION It will grow in most soil conditions. Fast-growing when young.
SITUATION Medium to large gardens.
HARDINESS Zone 4.

JUNIPERUS (CUPRESSACEAE)
JUNIPERS

The junipers are one of the larger genera of conifers. There are about 64 species, which between them have produced innumerable garden cultivars. They originate from the northern hemisphere, with the greatest concentration round the Mediterranean.

They are related to the *Cupressus*, and with their similar scaly leaves, the two are not always easy to tell apart. However, the difference is readily recognizable when you examine the fruit, as the junipers, in common with the yews, have a fleshy fruit. The basic cone-like structure is there, but the scales are fibrous or fleshy rather than hard and leathery as in the other conifers. These berries are used, while still green, to impart the characteristic flavour to gin. The berries have a lovely blue colour and birds are much attracted to them.

The leaves vary between their juvenile and mature states. The former are usually spiky, spreading, and carried in pairs or threes. As they mature they are likely to become scale-like and pressed against their stems. Although there is some variation in colour, they generally tend to be a bluish green. The shapes of the bush or tree of the various species and cultivars vary considerably. Some are loose, rounded bushes while others sprawl prostrate to the ground. Yet others rise in a tight vertical column. The sprawling varieties make an effective ground cover, while the upright ones are excellent as accents in the garden.

Most of the junipers are hardy, not too fussy about soils, and are easy to cultivate.

JUNIPERUS CHINENSIS 'AUREA'
GOLDEN CHINESE JUNIPER

This is a good shrub for any sized garden, either as a specimen or mixed in with other plants. It has a fine golden foliage which is neat, making a clean-cut plant. The shape varies from tall and columnar to more conical. Its slow growth and narrow shape make it suitable for a small garden.

ORIGIN Of garden origin.

MATURE HEIGHT 6m/20ft (10 years – 1.8m/6ft).

SHAPE Columnar to narrowly conical.

LEAVES Golden yellow but loses some of its brightness in winter.

CULTIVATION Avoid too much shade or the foliage turns green.

SITUATION Any size of garden.

HARDINESS Zone 6.

JUNIPERUS CHINENSIS 'KAIZUKA'
HOLLYWOOD JUNIPER

This is a very popular plant, perhaps more for its curiosity than its beauty. It has a rugged, craggy appearance, with everything seemingly out of line. It can be trained to have one leader or several. It can be made into a wonderful informal hedge. The foliage is bright green, dense, and soft to the touch. This tree is slow-growing.

ORIGIN Of garden origin from Japan.

MATURE HEIGHT 6m/20ft (10 years – 3m/10ft).

SHAPE Roughly pyramidal, but varies.

LEAVES Dense, showing the shape of the branches. Deep green.

CULTIVATION Will survive in either hot or cold areas. With care it can be shaped, but resist overdoing it.

SITUATION Any size of garden, although it will need replacing regularly in a small one.

HARDINESS Zone 5.

JUNIPERUS CHINENSIS *'PYRAMIDALIS'*
PYRAMIDAL CHINESE JUNIPER

This is a useful and popular garden plant. Its shape is broadly columnar, rather than pyramidal. The foliage remains in its juvenile stage, small and needlelike. It is soft when rubbed with an upward motion, but otherwise prickly. There is much confusion between this and *J.c.* 'Stricta', which closely resembles it.

ORIGIN Of garden origin in Japan.
MATURE HEIGHT 5m/16ft (10 years – 2m/6ft).
SHAPE Broadly columnar.
LEAVES Small, bluish green, sharp to the touch.
CULTIVATION No cultivation problems.
SITUATION Any size of garden, although it will need replacing in a small garden when it outgrows its situation.
HARDINESS Zone 5.

JUNIPERUS COMMUNIS *'COMPRESSA'*
COMPACT COMMON JUNIPER

'Compressa' is the ultimate rock garden conifer. It has a perfect, compact columnar shape, and grows very slowly, never becoming too big for a rock garden or a trough. The leaves are a grayish-green and of a small juvenile type. A splendid plant.

ORIGIN Pyrenees.
MATURE HEIGHT 90cm/3ft (10 years – 40cm/15in).
SHAPE Cigar shaped.
LEAVES Tiny, grayish green.
CULTIVATION Although hardy, it can suffer from wind and frost. Also has trouble with red spider mite. Trim out any wayward growths that some clones occasionally produce.
SITUATION Rock gardens, scree beds and troughs.
HARDINESS Zone 4.

JUNIPERUS COMMUNIS 'HIBERNICA'
IRISH JUNIPER

A columnar juniper, but of a much bigger stature than 'Compressa'. It makes a good plant wherever a pillar-like tree is needed in the garden. However, it is slow-growing and will take many years to reach a reasonable height. The foliage is a grayish green and is juvenile in form.
ORIGIN Ireland.
MATURE HEIGHT 5m/16ft (10 years – 1.8m/6ft).
SHAPE Tightly columnar.
LEAVES Juvenile, grayish green.
CULTIVATION Select your plant carefully, as some are looser-growing and not so tightly columnar. No clipping should be needed to keep its shape.
SITUATION Any size of garden.
HARDINESS Zone 4.

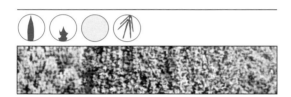

JUNIPERUS COMMUNIS 'MINIMA'
MINIMA COMMON JUNIPER

In contrast to the columnar forms, 'Minima' is a completely prostrate form of *J. communis*. The leaves are grayish green but covered with a bluish bloom. The underside has a band of silver stomata, which show in the twisted leaves. They are hard to the touch. The branches have a slight droop. This is not a very fast-spreading plant and it can be used on a rock garden.
ORIGIN Of garden origin.
MATURE HEIGHT 25cm/10in (10 years – 25cm/10in).
SHAPE Prostrate.
LEAVES Short needles, grayish green but with a bluish bloom, and silver on the reverse.
CULTIVATION No cultivation problems, but find the right position as the tree does not like being transplanted.
SITUATION Any size of garden.
HARDINESS Zone 4.

JUNIPERUS COMMUNIS 'REPANDA'
REPANDA JUNIPER

A prostrate juniper. It is much larger than 'Minima' and soon spreads to 2m/7ft or more. The leaves are soft to the touch and are close to their stems, giving the branches a neat, well-defined appearance. They are mid- to dark green. This plant grows too fast for all but the largest rock garden, but it does make good ground cover elsewhere.

ORIGIN Of garden origin.
MATURE HEIGHT 30cm/12in (10 years – 30cm/12in).
SHAPE Prostrate.
LEAVES Dull green.
CULTIVATION No problems in cultivation.
SITUATION Any size of garden.
HARDINESS Zone 4.

JUNIPERUS CONFERTA
SHORE JUNIPER

This mat-forming shrub from Japan grows in its natural habitat on the sea shore among sand dunes. It can be used as a rock garden plant and will weave its way in between the rocks. Its foliage is a little coarse, with prickly light-green leaves. Although it is a spreading shrub, a lot of the branchlets are erect.

ORIGIN Japan.
MATURE HEIGHT 30cm/12in (10 years – 30cm/12in).
SHAPE Prostrate.
LEAVES Stiff, light green, somewhat prickly.
CULTIVATION Although hardy, it is prone to frost damage.
SITUATION Large rock gardens.
HARDINESS Zone 5.

JUNIPERUS HORIZONTALIS 'BLUE CHIP'
BLUE CHIP JUNIPER

This is a prostrate juniper, with slightly erect stems, giving an attractive impression of broken water. The colour is also that of water, a good greenish blue. This is a moderately fast spreader that makes ideal ground cover.

ORIGIN Of garden origin in Denmark.
MATURE HEIGHT 25cm/10in (10 years – 25cm/10in).
SHAPE Prostrate.
LEAVES Greenish blue.
CULTIVATION The semi-erect nature of the stems make this tree a litter and leaf trap, so clean out regularly.
SITUATION Any size of garden, including large rock gardens.
HARDINESS Zone 5.

JUNIPERUS HORIZONTALIS 'PRINCE OF WALES'
PRINCE OF WALES JUNIPER

This is a very low-growing cultivar. The feathery foliage is bright green, slightly blue when young. Where the tips of the foliage are exposed to the weather in winter they turn purplish. The branches are very slightly erect, giving an overlapping layered effect. This is another good ground cover plant for a rock garden or bank.

ORIGIN Of garden origin in Canada.
MATURE HEIGHT 15cm/6in (10 years – 15cm/6in).
SHAPE Completely prostrate.
LEAVES Green; purplish in winter.
CULTIVATION No particular cultivation problems.
SITUATION Any size of garden. Medium to large rock gardens.
HARDINESS Zone 5.

JUNIPERUS HORIZONTALIS 'YOUNGSTOWN'
YOUNGSTOWN JUNIPER

One of the spreading junipers, but this one is low-growing rather than prostrate. Its branches are partially erect, forming a loose-knit bird's nest. The colour of the foliage is bright green, becoming purpler in winter in the colder areas. It is a good ground cover plant and makes a useful contrast to some of its more ground-hugging relatives.

ORIGIN Of garden origin.

MATURE HEIGHT 35cm/14in (10 years – 3cm/14in).

SHAPE Semi-erect, but spreading.

LEAVES Bright green, purple in winter.

CULTIVATION No problems in cultivation.

SITUATION Any size of garden. Suitable for medium to large rock gardens.

HARDINESS Zone 5.

JUNIPERUS X MEDIA 'BLAAUW'
BLAAUW'S JUNIPER

Unlike the other Media junipers, 'Blaauw' is an upright variety. It is a very dense plant, with the leading shoots sticking out at 50 degrees, giving the plant a rather bizarre, horned appearance. The foliage, which furnishes the branches tightly, is a good bluish gray. In spite of its short size, it makes a good plant to draw the eye.

ORIGIN Of garden origin in the Netherlands.

MATURE HEIGHT 2.5m/8ft (10 years – 1.5m/5ft).

SHAPE Upright with odd projections.

LEAVES A fine blue-gray.

CULTIVATION No problems as long as you do not cut off what may appear to be wayward growth.

SITUATION Any size of garden.

HARDINESS Zone 5.

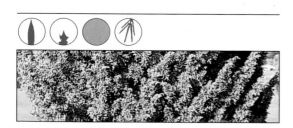

JUNIPERUS X MEDIA 'GOLD COAST'
GOLD COAST JUNIPER

This is a semi-prostrate form that makes a dense spreading plant. The tips of the branches are elegantly long, each dipped in gold. The colour intensifies in the winter. It is not a particularly fast grower, and although it can grow quite wide it is suitable for small as well as bigger gardens.

ORIGIN Of garden origin in the USA.
MATURE HEIGHT 4 feet (10 years – 3 feet).
SHAPE Low, spreading.
LEAVES Green, tipped with gold, green in the shade.
CULTIVATION No problems in cultivation.
SITUATION Any size of garden.
HARDINESS Zone 5.

JUNIPERUS X MEDIA 'PFITZERANA'
PFITZER JUNIPER

This is one of the most widely planted conifers. It is a moderately low-growing plant that bubbles up effusively in a spray of green-leaved branches. It is very dense and makes excellent ground cover, as well as an attractive feature. However, it eventually becomes very large, 4m/13ft or more across. There are several other cultivars.

ORIGIN Of garden origin in Germany.
MATURE HEIGHT 10 feet (10 years – 10 feet).
SHAPE Semi-erect, spreading.
LEAVES Green.
CULTIVATION The plant gets past its best after about ten years and it may be worth considering replacing it then.
SITUATION Medium to large gardens.
HARDINESS Zone 4.

JUNIPERUS SABINA 'TAMARISCIFOLIA'
TAMARISK-LEAVED JUNIPER

'Tamariscifolia' is a very old cultivar of *J. sabina*, having been in cultivation for over 200 years. Its horizontal branches make a wonderful low, spreading dome that is difficult to better. The foliage is a bright green. It is slow-spreading, but it is still probably too large for a small garden.

ORIGIN Of garden origin.

MATURE HEIGHT 60cm/2ft (10 years – 40cm/15in).

SHAPE A spreading dome.

LEAVES Bright green carried in overlapping sprays.

CULTIVATION Prone to juniper blight.

SITUATION Medium to large gardens.

HARDINESS Zone 5.

JUNIPERUS SCOPULORUM 'SKYROCKET'
SKYROCKET

This is a good name for this plant, as it well describes its narrow cigar shape, which is invaluable for giving a vertical emphasis to a garden. It is so narrow that it can be used in any size of garden, and makes a useful substitute in colder areas for the tall Mediterranean cedars. It is sometimes attributed to *J. virginiana*.

ORIGIN USA.

MATURE HEIGHT 8m/25ft (10 years – 2m/7ft).

SHAPE Very slender cigar-shape.

LEAVES Silvery blue.

CULTIVATION Easy to grow, but may become too large if grown in a rock garden, and may need eventual replacement. Cut out any untypical growth.

SITUATION Can be grown in any size of garden.

HARDINESS Zone 5.

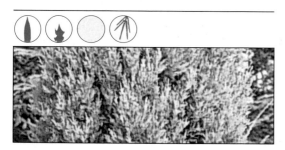

JUNIPERUS SQUAMATA 'BLUE STAR'
BLUE STAR JUNIPER

This is a good rich blue juniper that has a very compact growth. It forms a rounded shrub that is very slow-growing. 'Blue Star' makes an excellent plant for the rock garden. This cultivar was derived from compact shoots of *J.s.* 'Meyeri', which has the same colour foliage, but a more lax shape.

ORIGIN Of garden origin in the Netherlands.
MATURE HEIGHT 45cm/18in (10 years – 25cm/10in).
SHAPE Rounded, as wide as it is high.
LEAVES A good blue.
CULTIVATION No problems in cultivation.
SITUATION Any size of garden, particularly good on rock gardens.
HARDINESS Zone 5.

JUNIPERUS VIRGINIANA 'GREY OWL'
GREY OWL

'Grey Owl' is a spreading juniper that can be used as a ground cover plant as well as a decorative feature in its own right. The stems are yellow, and they contrast well with the silvery foliage. Some of the branches are ascending, so the plant can look a bit untidy. It needs plenty of room, as its eventual spread can be 5m/15ft or more.

ORIGIN The wild species is from North America, but the cultivar is of garden origin.
MATURE HEIGHT 90cm/3ft (10 years – 45cm/18in).
SHAPE A low, spreading plant.
LEAVES Small and pressed tight to the stems. Silvery gray, sometimes taking on a purplish tinge in winter.
CULTIVATION No problems in cultivation.
SITUATION Medium to large gardens. Can be used as a ground cover.
HARDINESS Zone 4.

LARIX (PINACEAE)
LARCHES

The most distinguishing feature about the larches is that they are deciduous. They are, in fact, the largest genus of deciduous conifers, with about 10 to 12 species. However, they are very closely related and often very difficult to tell apart. They are found throughout the northern hemisphere, usually as a pioneer species on the edge of the tree lines around the Arctic and on the upper slopes of mountains. This means that they are extremely hardy.

The foliage is of two types. On new shoots the needles are broad and spirally arranged. From the shoots' second year, the leaves are much narrower and are carried in rosettes. The leaves are soft and always a delight to run through the fingers.

Larches are usually grown as trees, although there are some dwarf forms.

LARIX DECIDUA
EUROPEAN LARCH

Larch is unusual in that it is deciduous and loses its leaves after a flush of autumnal colour. The spring growth is equally attractive, being a fresh light green, which offsets the wonderful colour of the young cones well. These are ultimately very tall trees, but there are various forms, including a weeping one, 'Pendula', and a dwarf one, 'Corley'.
ORIGIN Europe.
MATURE HEIGHT 50m/160ft (10 years – 6m/20ft).
SHAPE A tall open tree, broadly columnar.
LEAVES Deciduous. Light green in spring, golden in autumn.
CULTIVATION No problems in cultivation apart from the ultimate size.
SITUATION Large gardens and parkland.
HARDINESS Zone 2.

LARIX KAEMPFERI
JAPANESE LARCH

The Japanese larch is not greatly different from the European larch, except that it has waxy, red shoots. However, a number of forms can be found in cultivation in various parts of the world. There are several dwarf forms, some with blue foliage and others that are weeping. *L. leptolepsis* is now considered synonymous with – or as a form of – *L. kaempferi*.
ORIGIN Japan.
MATURE HEIGHT 30-100ft (10 years – 6m/20ft).
SHAPE Conventional, tall open structure that is roughly columnar.
LEAVES Deciduous, light green in spring, golden in autumn.
CULTIVATION Faster-growing and more tolerant of heavy soils than *L. decidua.*
SITUATION Large gardens and parkland. Smaller varieties are suitable for small gardens and rock gardens.
HARDINESS Zone 5.

METASEQUOIA (TAXODIACEAE)
DAWN REDWOOD

Like the *Ginkgo*, the *Metasequoia* is a relict from the past; and like that genus it also only has one species in existence today. Until the 1940s it was only known from fossil material and was thought to be extinct. Within seven years of being found in central China, it had been introduced into cultivation, and, although its existence in the wild is still precarious, it is now sufficiently widespread in gardens to avoid extinction. Redwoods make magnificent specimen trees of great beauty, and one must feel thankful that they were rescued. They look especially well when planted next to a pond or lake. They have rapid growth, especially when young, but this decreases markedly on a dry site after the tree has reached about 9m/30ft. Unfortunately redwoods are likely to grow too big for a small garden.

METASEQUOIA GLYPTOSTROBOIDES
DAWN REDWOOD

Once thought to be extinct, this "living fossil" was discovered in 1941 and is now widely seen in cultivation. It is a tree of great elegance and beauty. The trunk has a distinctive taper, and its bark is orangey-brown in colour. The foliage is very delicate. In many respects the dawn redwood is similar to the swamp cypress, *Taxodium distichium.*

ORIGIN South-western China.
MATURE HEIGHT 18m/60ft (10 years – 4m/13ft).
SHAPE A slender, cone-shaped tree.
LEAVES Deciduous, leaves appearing in late spring. They are feathery, pale green, and take on beautiful autumn colours.
CULTIVATION This tree likes a moist habitat, preferably near water. It grows rapidly to start with, and then slows down.
SITUATION Medium to large gardens.
HARDINESS Zone 6.

PICEA (PINACEAE)
SPRUCES

The spruces are popular in cultivation, both as an economic crop (for pulp and Christmas trees), and as ornamental plants. There are about 37 species which occur throughout the northern hemisphere. In cultivation there is a large number of cultivars.

The leaves are needlelike, hard, and often prickly. They grow singly and not in bunches. When allowed to die naturally (they have a four-year life), they leave behind a small peg-like projection. As the tree ages, the accumulation of these old projections makes the stems very rough, a distinctive characteristic of spruces. The leaves are carried spirally on the shoot, but parted underneath so that they appear to grow only on either side. The leaf colour is usually a bright green, but in cultivation there are many variants available. New growth in the spring is much lighter in colour and brightens up the appearance of the tree, often giving it a speckled appearance. The young cones are erect until they have been pollinated, then they hang down. They ripen in autumn and have the decorative benefit of remaining intact.

In the wild, species grow as trees, normally with a typical Christmas-tree shape, but in cultivation they come in all shapes and sizes. They can be grown as part of a larger planting or can be used as specimen trees. There are also ground-hugging cultivars that make good ground cover, and others which form small rounded hummocks, and are ideal for rock gardens or even for growing in troughs.

PICEA ABIES 'INVERSA'
DROOPING NORWAY SPRUCE

This is a very odd plant that is curious rather than beautiful. Its natural tendency is to droop. If it is allowed to do this on the ground, it becomes a spreading prostrate shrub. However, if it is staked early in its life, it can be trained into an upright tree with a hang-dog expression and pendulous branches.

ORIGIN Of garden origin.
MATURE HEIGHT 15m/50ft (10 years – 3m/10ft depending on training).
SHAPE Pendulous pyramid.
LEAVES Light green.
CULTIVATION Needs to be trained if you want an upright plant.
SITUATION Medium to large gardens.
HARDINESS Zone 4.

PICEA ABIES 'MUCRONATA'
MUCRONATA SPRUCE

'Mucronata' is a very old cultivar, at least 150 years old. It forms a very regular, conical tree, in which the branches and foliage are very dense. The branches have a steep upward sweep, which helps to define the tree's precise shape. The colour of the leaves is a bright bluish green.

ORIGIN Of garden origin in France.
MATURE HEIGHT 5m/16ft (10 years – 1.2m/4ft).
SHAPE Conical.
LEAVES Bright blue-green; very dense.
CULTIVATION No problems in cultivation.
SITUATION Suitable for medium- and large-sized gardens.
HARDINESS Zone 4.

P I C E A   A B I E S
'*P E N D U L A   M A J O R* '
PENDULOUS NORWAY SPRUCE

Trees do not have to be beautiful to be interesting. This is certainly a
curious form, with all the subsidiary branches hanging from the main
ones, resembling limp pieces of rope or rag. The whole tree looks a bit
like a scarecrow. However, the tree does have its charm and is well
worth growing if you have the space.

ORIGIN Norway.
MATURE HEIGHT 20m/65ft (10 years – 7m/23ft).
SHAPE Loosely pyramidal.
LEAVES Dark green.
CULTIVATION No problems in cultivation except possibly ultimate size
if space is short.
SITUATION Medium to large gardens.
HARDINESS Zone 4.

P I C E A   A B I E S
'*R E F L E X A* '
WEEPING NORWAY SPRUCE

This is a magnificent plant that can be trained in at
least two different ways. The first is to let it sprawl
across the ground, preferably down a rock garden,
while the second is to train the main stem vertically
for a short distance before letting the tree revert to its
natural weeping position. The young pale green
growth is very attractive.

ORIGIN Of garden origin.
MATURE HEIGHT Depends on how the plant is
trained.
SHAPE Prostrate or pendulous.
LEAVES Dark green, with light green young growth
in spring.
CULTIVATION Train this tree to whatever height you
require.
SITUATION Small to large gardens. Suitable for large
rockeries.
HARDINESS Zone 4.

PICEA BREWERIANA
BREWER'S WEEPING SPRUCE

This weeping spruce is one of the most beautiful of all conifers with its pendulous branches, from which hang the foliage branches, like cobwebs in a forgotten forest. When the tree is young the main branches are held more erect, but the overall effect is still the same. The foliage is dark green, which adds to the beauty.

ORIGIN Western North America.
MATURE HEIGHT 30m/100ft (10 years – 3m/10ft).
SHAPE Decidedly pendulous.
LEAVES Dark green, with paler young growth in spring.
CULTIVATION No problems in cultivation except for its ultimate size.
SITUATION Large gardens and parkland. Can be used in smaller gardens if replaced after 10 to 15 years.
HARDINESS Zone 2.

PICEA GLAUCA 'ALBERTA CONICA'
DWARF ALBERTA SPRUCE

This is a very slow-growing conifer that forms a dense, conical tree. It is so compact that it is impossible to see any branches below the foliage. It is slow enough to be grown in the rock garden, but its eventual size makes it more suitable for the open garden. It contrasts well with looser-growing and prostrate conifers.

ORIGIN Originally found as a wild plant in Alberta, Canada.
MATURE HEIGHT 3m/10ft (10 years – 75cm/30in).
SHAPE Conical.
LEAVES Bright grass green, with lighter buds.
CULTIVATION This plant can be trimmed to keep it small if required.
SITUATION Large rock garden or small garden.
HARDINESS Zone 4.

P I C E A   O M O R I K A
SERBIAN SPRUCE

The Serbian spruce is one of the most elegant of the conifers. It grows in a tall, narrow spire, gently tapering as it rises. The branches at the top are ascending, but the longer basal ones become more pendulous. The foliage is a good dark brown and the cones turn purplish blue before ripening. Dwarf forms are available.

ORIGIN Former Yugoslavia.
MATURE HEIGHT 30m/100ft (10 years – 6m/20ft).
SHAPE A tapering pyramid.
LEAVES Dark green.
CULTIVATION No problems in cultivation if you have the space.
SITUATION Large gardens and parkland.
HARDINESS Zone 4.

P I C E A   P U N G E N S '*G L O B O S A*'
GLOBOSA BLUE SPRUCE

This is a superb plant for the rock garden. It makes a compact shrub with a wonderful blue foliage. The general shape is a miniature globe, somewhat flattened on the top. It may well be the same plant as that called *P.p.* 'Montgomery', which is very similar in appearance.

ORIGIN Of garden origin in the Netherlands.
MATURE HEIGHT 75cm/30in (10 years – 50cm/20in).
SHAPE Spherical.
LEAVES Stiff. Steely blue.
CULTIVATION In warmer regions, the tree can be defoliated by miles. Spray regularly with water.
SITUATION Any size of garden. Ideal for rock gardens and scree beds.
HARDINESS Zone 3.

PINUS (PINACEAE)
PINES

The pines are the largest genus of conifers, with nearly 100 species. They come from the northern hemisphere, from the warm Mediterranean and the West Indies, and from the colder north, but they grow mainly at higher altitudes, so most are hardy in cultivation.

The pines are characterized by their needlelike leaves, some very long (up to 25cm/10in or more). The leaves are held in bundles (fascicles) of two, three, or five, depending on the species. The base of each bundle is held in a short sleeve. In section, each fascicle is a circle, with the individual leaves contributing a segment. Young plants produce a different type of juvenile leaf. These are toothed, solitary, and arranged spirally. The young shoots appear as attractive "candles" set in a cluster of leaves. The cones are woody and vary in shape from spherical to elongated – up to 45cm/18in in some species. The seed is usually winged for wind dispersal.

These trees vary from the tall elegance of a Scots pine to a spreading shape. Some, such as *P. mugo*, develop into shrubs rather than trees, and there are plenty of cultivars that will suit a small garden or even a rock garden.

PINUS ARISTATA
BRISTLECONE PINE

The bristlecones are the oldest trees in the world, some living up to 5,000 years. Needless to say, they are extremely slow-growing, although the growth rate varies, with some plants growing as much as 13ft/13.9m in 40 years. However, this is still slow to most gardeners. These pines make good rock garden plants in their first 20 to 30 years.

ORIGIN Colorado, New Mexico, and Arizona.
MATURE HEIGHT 15m/50ft (10 years – 60cm/2ft).
SHAPE Irregularly conical.
LEAVES Dense brushes of dark needles.
CULTIVATION Patience is required.
SITUATION Any size of garden. Ideal for rock gardens for the first 20 years.
HARDINESS Zone 5.

PINUS ARMANII
ARMANI PINE

This is a wonderfully graceful pine, with huge tassels of long needles held in groups of five. The needles are deep green, but their inner face has a white bloom, giving a general impression of pale green. The trees grow very big, too big for the average garden, but make magnificent specimen trees where there is space.

ORIGIN Tibet and China.

MATURE HEIGHT 40m/130ft (10 years – 7.5m/25ft).

SHAPE Spreading pyramidal.

LEAVES General appearance is a pale green.

CULTIVATION No problems apart from size.

SITUATION Large gardens and parkland.

HARDINESS Zone 7.

PINUS DENSIFLORUS 'UMBRACULIFERA'
UMBRELLA PINE

This is a delightful tree for the small garden. There are various forms in cultivation. Some form a dome, like an umbrella (including the ribs, represented by the branches reaching down from the canopy to the trunk), while others make a more rounded shape. They are slow-growing and very decorative at all stages of their life.

ORIGIN From the wild in Japan.

MATURE HEIGHT 5m/16ft (10 years – 90cm/3ft).

SHAPE Rounded but spreading.

LEAVES Rich green needles, carried in pairs.

CULTIVATION No problems in cultivation.

SITUATION Any size of garden.

HARDINESS Zone 4.

PINUS LEUCODERMIS
BOSNIAN PINE

This is a well-shaped pine of attractive appearance. It is conical in shape and is clothed in dark green foliage, which is held in distinctive whorls. Further attraction is given by the young white shoots, which look like candles, and by the beautiful cobalt blue cones. There are several cultivars, including the Schmidt's pine. Although the Bosnian pine eventually becomes large, it is quite slow-growing.

ORIGIN Western Balkans.
MATURE HEIGHT 30m/100ft (10 years – 3m/10ft).
SHAPE Pyramidal.
LEAVES Dark green in dense whorls. A two-needle species.
CULTIVATION No problems in cultivation.
SITUATION Large gardens and parkland.
HARDINESS Zone 6.

PINUS LEUCODERMIS 'SCHMIDTII'
SCHMIDT'S BOSNIAN PINE

Dwarf pines have a wonderful fascination for many gardeners, and this is one of the smallest. It is of wild origin, and although the original plant was over 100 years old, it was still less than 3m/10ft tall. In cultivation it is even more compact. The leaves have all the characteristics of a normal pine. It does not produce cones. This really is a delightful plant.

ORIGIN Near Sarajevo, former Yugoslavia.
MATURE HEIGHT 60cm/2ft (10 years – 23cm/8in).
SHAPE Rounded.
LEAVES The needles are dark green in groups of two.
CULTIVATION No difficulty as long as the soil is not allowed to dry out before the tree has become established.
SITUATION Perfect for the rock garden.
HARDINESS Zone 5.

P I N U S   M U G O
DWARF MOUNTAIN PINE

This is a very useful species for those who only have a small garden. It is a very variable plant but, unlike most pines, it usually tends to have several main stems instead of one trunk. The trees are quite loose-growing and frequently used as "avalanche brakes" in the mountains. There are also several cultivars available.

ORIGIN Europe.
MATURE HEIGHT 3.5m/12ft (10 years – 2m/7ft).
SHAPE Roundish with a flat top.
LEAVES Two-needle species of a dark bluish green coloration.
CULTIVATION No problems in cultivation.
SITUATION Any size of garden. Good for banks and rough ground.
HARDINESS Zone 2.

P I N U S   M U G O   ' H U M P Y '
HUMPY MOUNTAIN PINE

A very small cultivar that forms a squat, slightly spreading mound. It is very slow-growing, making it ideal for even a small rock garden. The small leaves are dark green, brightened in winter by the tiny red buds of the following year's growth. This cultivar has a lot to recommend it.

ORIGIN Of garden origin in the Netherlands.
MATURE HEIGHT 60cm/2ft (10 years – 30cm/12in).
SHAPE Flattish, rounded bush.
LEAVES Small, dark green, and carried in pairs.
CULTIVATION No problems in cultivation.
SITUATION Any size of garden. Good for rock gardens.
HARDINESS Zone 2.

PINUS MUGO 'MOPS'
MOPS MOUNTAIN PINE

A celebrated miniature pine. It is not as small-growing or as compact as the Humpy mountain pine, but it is still a splendid plant. It can be grown on any rock garden in its early years, but eventually it will only be suitable for medium and large-sized beds. The leaves are darkish blue-green and carried in pairs.

ORIGIN Of garden origin in the Netherlands.
MATURE HEIGHT 1.2m/4ft (10 years – 45cm/18in).
SHAPE More rounded than 'Humpy'.
LEAVES Dark blue-green.
CULTIVATION No problems in cultivation.
SITUATION Rock gardens of any size, especially medium to large ones.
HARDINESS Zone 2.

PINUS NIGRA
BLACK PINE

There are several botanical subspecies of this large tree, named after their wild location: the Austrian, Corsican, and Dalmation pines, for example. They are all only slightly different from each other. The Corsican is the fastest-growing, while the Austrian is good planted next to the sea. There is also a number of dwarf and variegated forms.
ORIGIN Europe.
MATURE HEIGHT 40m/130ft (10 years – 3m/10ft).
SHAPE Broadly conical.
LEAVES Dark green and carried in pairs.
CULTIVATION No problems in cultivation. Makes a good shelter-belt.
SITUATION Medium-sized gardens when young, later, larger gardens and parkland.
HARDINESS Zone 4.

PINUS NIGRA 'GLOBOSA'
GLOBOSA BLACK PINE

While the main species of the black pine can be rather formidable for the small garden, its cultivar, 'Globosa', has rather a lot to offer. It forms a dwarf tree with a rounded shape, becoming pyramidal in time – a perfect miniature pine. The well-known form 'Hornibrookiana' is also dwarf, but lower and more spreading.

ORIGIN Of garden origin.
MATURE HEIGHT 43/10ft (10 years – 90cm/3ft).
SHAPE Rounded, becoming more pyramidal with age.
LEAVES Dark green, borne in pairs.
CULTIVATION No problems in cultivation.
SITUATION Any size of garden, including large rock gardens.
HARDINESS Zone 4.

PINUS PARVIFLORA
JAPANESE WHITE PINE

This plant has been in cultivation for a very long time, and as one would expect there is now a considerable number of cultivars, including many with Japanese names. Although it is broadly conical in shape, the forms in cultivation are usually much lower and spreading. The foliage is deep green with whitish blue on the inner face of each leaf.

ORIGIN Japan.
MATURE HEIGHT 12m/40ft (10 years – 3m/10ft).
SHAPE Conical or spreading.
LEAVES Mixture of dark green and whitish blue. Carried in fives in beautiful, twisted whorls.
CULTIVATION No difficulties in cultivation.
SITUATION Medium to large gardens.
HARDINESS Zone 5.

PINUS PARVIFLORA 'GLAUCA'
GLAUCOUS JAPANESE WHITE PINE

This probably is the most popular of the *P. parviflora* cultivars. Its popularity stems from its wonderful blue foliage, which, like that of its parent, is carried in whorled bunches. It is a slow-growing tree, and although it is not very large in its formative years, it will eventually become very big. This tree cones freely.

ORIGIN Of garden origin.

MATURE HEIGHT 10m/30ft (10 years – 2m/7ft).

SHAPE Spreading pyramidal.

LEAVES Blue, with the needles carried in fives.

CULTIVATION No problems in cultivation. Can be pruned to keep it in shape.

SITUATION Medium to large gardens.

HARDINESS Zone 5.

PINUS PONDEROSA
WESTERN YELLOW PINE

The western yellow pine will eventually make a massive tree, but in its early stages it is of comparatively slow growth and can even be used in small gardens as long as it is removed before it gets too big. The foliage is a grayish or yellowish green, and is carried in flattened whorls, giving the young trees a very attractive appearance.

ORIGIN Western side of the Rocky Mountains, USA.

MATURE HEIGHT 40m/130ft (10 years – 3m/10ft).

SHAPE Broadly pyramidal.

LEAVES Grayish green, usually carried in threes.

CULTIVATION No problems in cultivation except that it will eventually become very big.

SITUATION Medium to large gardens.

HARDINESS Zone 4.

PINUS PUMILA
DWARF SIBERIAN PINE

Also called the Japanese pine, this is usually a prostrate shrub, although it can grow into a tree of up to 6m/20ft. However, like many pines, it will remain dwarf and suitable for a rock garden before eventually outgrowing its position. This species has a very attractive bluish green foliage and red-purple young cones.

ORIGIN Eastern Asia.
MATURE HEIGHT 6m/20ft (10 years – 60cm/2ft).
SHAPE Either upright and pyramidal, or more usually prostrate and spreading.
LEAVES Blue-green. Carried in fives.
CULTIVATION No problems in cultivation.
SITUATION Any size of garden including large rock gardens for the first 20 years.
HARDINESS Zone 5.

PINUS PUMILA 'GLAUCA'
GLAUCOUS DWARF SIBERIAN PINE

This is similar in appearance to *P. pumila,* but it is on an even smaller scale, rarely reaching much above 60cm/2ft in its lifetime. This makes it an ideal plant for a rock garden, although in its early life it is almost small enough to be grown in a trough. Its blue foliage gives it the alternative name of 'Blue Dwarf'.

ORIGIN Of garden origin.
MATURE HEIGHT 60cm/2ft (10 years – 25cm/10in).
SHAPE Spreading but sometimes with a positive leader.
LEAVES Bluish. Carried in fives.
CULTIVATION No problems in cultivation.
SITUATION Any size of garden. Ideal for rock gardens.
HARDINESS Zone 5.

PINUS STROBUS 'RADIATUS'
DWARF WEYMOUTH PINE

'Radiatus', or 'Nanus' as it is also called, is the most popular form of this pine. Although its eventual height makes it suitable for a large rock garden, its slow initial growth allows it to be grown in a small garden. The growth is quite dense, giving the impression of a billowing cloud of pine needles.
ORIGIN Of garden origin.
MATURE HEIGHT 2m/7ft (10 years – 60cm/2ft).
SHAPE Broadly conical.
LEAVES Bluish green. Carried in fives.
CULTIVATION No problems in cultivation.
SITUATION Any size of garden, including rock gardens.
HARDINESS Zone 3.

PINUS SYLVESTRIS
SCOTS PINE

This is a magnificent tree, which eventually becomes too large for anything other than a large garden. However, while it is young it can be grown in a smaller garden and there are plenty of cultivars that remain small. However, if there is space, this tree is well worth growing for its grace and poise.
ORIGIN Northern hemisphere.
MATURE HEIGHT 30m/100ft (10 years – 3m/10ft).
SHAPE Pyramidal when young.
LEAVES Bluish green. Carried in pairs.
CULTIVATION Not too happy on wet or very chalky soils.
SITUATION Any size of garden when young, but only large gardens when older.
HARDINESS Zone 2.

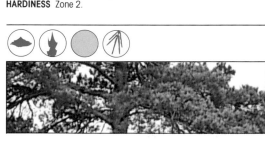

PINUS SYLVESTRIS 'BEUVRONENSIS'
BEUVRONENSIS SCOTS PINE

This is one of the smallest of the Scots pines, eventually rising to barely 45cm/18in. It is extremely slow-growing, forming a very compact plant in which the foliage completely hides the branches. It is derived from a witches' broom, which the Scots pine is notorious for producing.

ORIGIN Of garden origin.
MATURE HEIGHT 45cm/18in (10 years – 5cm/6in).
SHAPE Rounded bush.
LEAVES Bluish green. Carried in pairs.
CULTIVATION Takes some time to reach planting out size, and needs regular potting.
SITUATION In the early stages this plant may be too small to plant out, but will make a good trough plant.
HARDINESS Zone 2.

PINUS SYLVESTRIS 'MOSERI'
MOSER'S SCOTS PINE

This is a truly magnificent plant. It forms a miniature tree with a rounded shape covered in dense clouds of foliage. Older trees have a very Japanese look. It is short-trunked and so is more of a shrub than a tree. 'Moseri' is sometimes listed as a cultivar of *P. nigra*.

ORIGIN Of garden origin.
MATURE HEIGHT 3m/10ft (10 years – 60cm/2ft).
SHAPE A rounded bush-like appearance.
LEAVES Green. Carried in bunches of two.
CULTIVATION No problems in cultivation.
SITUATION Any size of garden.
HARDINESS Zone 2.

PODOCARPUS (PODOCARPACEAE)
PODOCARPS

In spite of not being very common in cultivation, the podocarps are, in fact, the second largest genus of conifers. They originate mainly in the tropics, and mainly in the southern hemisphere. Although some eventually form large trees, several make very decorative shrubs, some even small enough to be grown on rock gardens.

The foliage is strap-like, often quite broad. It is leathery and can be prickly. In some species the foliage takes on a different colour in winter. The plants are dioecious, needing both male and female plants to produce seed. The cones are fruit-like and edible in some species. Seed is not generally produced in the cooler climates.

PODOCARPUS ACUTIFOLIA
POINTED-LEAF PODOCARP

Although the normal form of this podocarp grows to 10m/30ft or more, it is usually grown in gardens as a shrub, pruned as necessary to keep it down to size. It then makes a low spreading shrub. It can also be used as a hedge that needs trimming only once a year. The foliage is a bronzed light green.

ORIGIN New Zealand.

MATURE HEIGHT 10m/30ft (10 years – 45cm/18in).

SHAPE Low and spreading.

LEAVES Bronzed green; browner in winter.

CULTIVATION Keep pruned to retain low height.

SITUATION Any size of garden.

HARDINESS Zone 6.

P O D O C A R P U S N I V A L I S
ALPINE PODOCARP

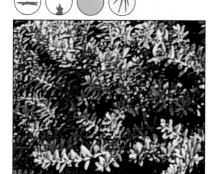

This is not one of the taller trees in this genus. Even in the wild it only forms a low-growing bush, perhaps growing up to about 90cm/3ft. In cultivation it is still low-growing, but can become somewhat looser. However, it can easily be pruned if necessary. There are ground-hugging forms. The foliage is a soft olive green, but there are also bronze-leaved cultivars. Its dense spreading qualities make it an ideal ground cover.

ORIGIN New Zealand.
MATURE HEIGHT 2m/7ft (10 years 60cm/2ft).
SHAPE Prostrate, sometimes rising in the centre to a slight cone.
LEAVES Olive green.
CULTIVATION Can be grown on chalky soils. Will grow well in shade.
SITUATION Any size of garden, including rock gardens.
HARDINESS Zone 6.

PSEUDOTSUGA (PINACEAE)
DOUGLAS FIRS

The Douglas firs are related to the spruces *(Picea)* and the hemlocks *(Tsuga)*. They are mainly forest trees of some size, but there are garden forms that are of quite low stature. Depending on which botanists you follow there are either six or twenty different species, of which *P. menziesii* (and its many cultivars) is about the only one in general cultivation. The leaves are green and are set directly into small depressions on their shoots. The cones are carried in an erect position until they are pollinated, after which they hang down. They do not break up when the seed is shed. The majority of species are too big for cultivation and have no special qualities to promote them. However, the various cultivars are well worth growing and some are suitable even for small gardens.

PSEUDOTSUGA MENZIESII 'FLETCHERI'
FLETCHER'S DOUGLAS FIR

Unlike the species, this is a very slow-growing tree that rarely makes anything larger than a shrub. It forms a low, spreading plant that is wider than it is tall. The foliage is dark green, but is peppered in spring with new growth. It makes an excellent specimen tree.

ORIGIN Of garden origin.
MATURE HEIGHT 3m/10ft (10 years – 60cm/2ft).
SHAPE Spreading.
LEAVES Dark green with a touch of blue.
CULTIVATION No cultivation problems.
SITUATION Any size of garden.
HARDINESS Zone 6.

PSEUDOTSUGA MENZIESII '*GLAUCA*'
BLUE DOUGLAS FIR

This is generally thought to be a natural variety of *P. menziesii*, but occasionally it is seen as a species in its own right. It does not, perhaps, make such a stately tree as the main species, but its blue foliage makes it an attractive plant. The cones are smaller and have a more interesting shape.

ORIGIN Western USA.
MATURE HEIGHT 60m/200ft (10 years – 6m/20ft).
SHAPE Broadly conical.
LEAVES Glaucous blue.
CULTIVATION No problems in cultivation except for its ultimate size.
SITUATION Large gardens and parkland.
HARDINESS Zone 6.

PSEUDOTSUGA MENZIESII '*LITTLE JON*'
LITTLE JON DOUGLAS FIR

The Douglas firs are enormous trees, and, beautiful as they are, not suitable for small or medium gardens. However, there is one delightful small version that would suit any situation. It forms a very slow-growing, pyramidal tree that never gets very big. The leaves are small and a light to mid green in colour.

ORIGIN Of wild origin in Pennsylvania, USA.
MATURE HEIGHT 1.2m/4ft (10 years – 45cm/18in).
SHAPE Pyramidal.
LEAVES Light to mid-green.
CULTIVATION No problems in cultivation.
SITUATION Any size of garden, including rock gardens.
HARDINESS Zone 6.

SEQUOIA (TAXODIACEAE)
COASTAL REDWOOD

This is a one-species genus, *S. sempervirens* being the only member.
It is restricted to a narrow strip of Pacific coastline in North America.
However, it is known from fossil material to have grown in other areas
of the world. The moist atmosphere caused by the frequent sea fogs seems
to have something to do with its present narrow distribution.
In cultivation it does best where the atmosphere is moist and not too
exposed to drying winds.
This redwood has the reputation of being the tallest tree in the world,
112m/367ft being the record, so these are not trees for small gardens.
Unlike most other conifers, this tree will resprout from the remaining
stump if it is cut to the ground.

SEQUOIA SEMPERVIRENS
COASTAL REDWOOD

This is the only species in the genus. It is an extremely quick-
growing tree, ultimately reaching great heights. However, it
can be coppiced, which means that if grown in a small
garden, it can be cut down so that it sprouts again, thus
always keeping it within bounds. The leaves are flat and
arranged along either side of the shoot, much in the manner
of yews.

ORIGIN Pacific Coast of the USA.
MATURE HEIGHT 45m/150ft (10 years – 7.5m/25ft).
SHAPE Pyramidal.
LEAVES Flat and strap-like. Dark green.
CULTIVATION Needs regular coppicing if you wish to keep it
under control. Foliage burns if exposed to cold winds.
SITUATION Suited really only to large gardens and parkland,
unless coppiced.
HARDINESS Zone 7.

SEQUOIADENDRON (TAXODIACEAE)
WELLINGTONIA

This is a single-species genus, *S. giganteum* being the sole representative. It is very similar to the *Sequoia,* and at one stage was considered to be part of that genus. However, it differs in its leaves, which are more scale-like, and it has larger cones. Wellingtonia also make very tall trees, the largest existing one is 100m/330ft tall and 12m/40ft in diameter. Some trees live up to 3,500 years, making them a good investment. They are very restricted, in the wild, to part of the Sierra Nevada in California. The bark is soft, but very thick. It is able to withstand fire.

SEQUOIADENDRON GIGANTEUM
WELLINGTONIA

These remarkable trees are tougher than their close relatives, the *Sequoia,* but they grow just as big. They are also fast-growing but, unlike the *Sequoia* they cannot be coppiced, so are not at all suitable for a small or medium garden. The foliage is gray-green and scale like. This tree needs space to be seen at its best.

ORIGIN Sierra Nevada, California.
MATURE HEIGHT 50m/160ft (10 years 7.5m/25ft).
SHAPE Pyramidal.
LEAVES Gray, small, and scale-like.
CULTIVATION Prefers a moist, rich soil.
SITUATION Large gardens and parkland.
HARDINESS Zone 6.

TAXUS (TAXODIACEAE)
YEWS

The yews consist of eight or nine species, of which fewer than half are in
general cultivation. However, the commonest species, *Taxus baccata,* has
provided gardens with very many cultivars of various sorts.
They have strap-like leaves arranged in flat rows on either side of the stem.
They generally form a broadly pyramidal tree, but there are many other
shapes available. One distinct feature is the seed capsule, which is a juicy
red fruit, known as an aril. It looks completely unlike the more typical
cones of other conifers, but there are, in fact, distinct botanical
similarities.
Yews, in particular *T. baccata,* have been in cultivation for many centuries.
As with most plants of that length of history, they are tightly bound up
with European folklore. Their timber was much favoured for long-bows.
As trees and shrubs, their slow-growing and dense nature has made them
ideal for hedges and topiary.

TAXUS BACCATA
ENGLISH YEW

Yew is possibly the most versatile of all
conifers. It comes in all sizes, shapes and
colours, and can be used as specimen plants,
or background. It is excellent for shaping into
topiary or hedges. It is slow-growing but the
wait is always very worth while. The species
has dark green leaves. Male and female
flowers are carried on different trees.
ORIGIN Europe.
MATURE HEIGHT 10m/33ft (10 years –
3m/10ft).
SHAPE Rounded, but can be trimmed to any
shape.
LEAVES Dark-green, flat needles.
CULTIVATION Will grow on chalk and in the
shade. Poisonous to livestock.
SITUATION If trimmed, any size of garden.
HARDINESS Zone 6.

TAXUS BACCATA 'FASTIGIATA ROBUSTA'
ROBUSTA IRISH YEW

There are several fastigiate yews, all, as their name suggests, have an upright growth. 'Robusta' is the most fastigiate of the lot. It is a slender column of branches tightly pressed against the trunk. The green foliage is the same as any normal yew and it produces red berries. It makes a wonderful focal point.

ORIGIN Of garden origin.
MATURE HEIGHT 3.5m/12ft (10 years – 2m/7ft).
SHAPE Distinctly columnar.
LEAVES Dark green.
CULTIVATION Remove any wayward branches.
SITUATION Any size of garden.
HARDINESS Zone 6.

TAXUS BACCATA 'SEMPERAUREA'
EVERGOLD YEW

Not all yews have the conventional dark green foliage. 'Semperaurea' is one of a number with golden leaves. This is a loose bushy form. It is very slow-growing and never gets very tall, although it can become quite broad. It can, of course, be cut back in a small garden to keep it within bounds.

ORIGIN Of garden origin.
MATURE HEIGHT 2.5m/8ft (10 years – 1.2m/4ft).
SHAPE Loose, rounded bush.
LEAVES Golden yellow, greener toward the centre and under the bush.
CULTIVATION No problems in cultivation.
SITUATION Any size of garden, including rock gardens if it is kept trimmed.
HARDINESS Zone 6.

TAXUS BACCATA 'STANDISHII'
STANDISH'S YEW

This is a good garden form, especially for those who only have a small garden. It forms a good columnar shape and has arguably the best golden foliage of any yew. The disadvantage is that it is very slow-growing, so will take 20 or 30 years to make a reasonably tall tree, growing up to 1.5m/5ft..

ORIGIN Of garden origin.
MATURE HEIGHT 2m/7ft (10 years – 75cm/30in).
SHAPE Columnar.
LEAVES Standard yew leaves, but a golden-yellow.
CULTIVATION No problems in cultivation.
SITUATION Any size of garden, including rock gardens.
HARDINESS Zone 6.

THUJA (CUPRESSACEAE)
THUJA

This small genus of only five or six species is important in cultivation as it has produced a large number of ornamental cultivars. The leaves are scale-like, pressed tightly to the branches and are carried in flat sprays. Many of the decorative forms are of a golden or greeny-golden nature. A characteristic of these trees is that if the foliage is crushed it has a strong scent. Cones are small and somewhat elongated.

Thuja generally make rather large trees, but there are more than enough smaller versions from which to choose. They are highly decorative and make good specimen trees. They can be clipped and kept in shape and so can be used as hedging plants. However, they need more attention than yew.

THUJA OCCIDENTALIS 'AUREA'
GOLDEN ARBORVITAE

There are several golden forms of *T. occidentalis.* This is one for people with a larger garden. It has superb golden foliage, which shines out like a beacon. Although it looks best against green trees and shrubs, it should not be planted in shade, or the golden colour turns to green. It makes a very good specimen plant.

ORIGIN Of garden origin.
MATURE HEIGHT 12m/40ft (10 years – 4.5m/15ft).
SHAPE Pyramidal.
LEAVES Golden yellow.
CULTIVATION No problems in cultivation apart from its ultimate size.
SITUATION Medium to large gardens.
HARDINESS Zone 5.

THUJA OCCIDENTALIS 'ELLWANGERIANA AUREA'

ELLWANGERIANA AUREA ARBORVITAE

This forms a roundish bush of golden foliage. It has several leaders, but as it ages it becomes more pyramidal in shape. Early in its life it is very similar in colour and shape to the popular 'Rheingold'. However, as they age 'Ellwangeriana Aurea' grows away and becomes the taller of the two. They are frequently confused in nurseries and plant centres.

ORIGIN Of garden origin.

MATURE HEIGHT 4m/13ft (10 years – 75cm/30in).

SHAPE Rounded, becoming pyramidal.

LEAVES Golden. Sprays slightly smaller than 'Rheingold'.

CULTIVATION No problems in cultivation.

SITUATION Any size of garden, although it will eventually become too large for rock gardens.

HARDINESS Zone 4.

THUJA OCCIDENTALIS 'LUTEA NANA'

DWARF YELLOW ARBORVITAE

Not surprisingly, this is a popular shrub. It is one of the oldest golden-leaf varieties and has stayed the test of time well. The young foliage is a creamy yellow, which matures, as the season progresses, to gold, and eventually takes on a more bronzy hue. A plant for all seasons, helped by the fact that it is extremely hardy.

ORIGIN Of garden origin.

MATURE HEIGHT 4m/13ft (10 years – 2m/7ft).

SHAPE Loosely round when young, but developing into a narrow pyramid.

LEAVES Golden yellow.

CULTIVATION Plant in the open, away from shade.

SITUATION Any size of garden.

HARDINESS Zone 4.

THUJA ORIENTALIS
'AUREA NANA'
GOLDEN DWARF ARBORVITAE

Thuja orientalis is distinct from the other thujas in that the flat sprays of leaves are noticeably held vertically. They are also scentless when crushed. 'Aurea Nana' forms a well-shaped bush, in which the vertical leaves are very noticeable. It is sometimes known as 'Berkmann's Golden Biota'.

ORIGIN Of garden origin.
MATURE HEIGHT 90cm/3ft (10 years – 60cm/2ft).
SHAPE Ovoid or a rounded pillar.
LEAVES Golden, greener in winter. Held in the vertical plane.
CULTIVATION No problems in cultivation.
SITUATION Any size of garden.
HARDINESS Zone 6.

THUJA ORIENTALIS
'SIEBOLDII'
SIEBOLD'S ARBORVITAE

'Sieboldii' is a very old form of *T. orientalis*. It forms a very densely packed conical shrub in which all the foliage sprays are held vertically. The spring growth is a golden colour, but this changes to a bright green as the seasons progress. This shrub makes a good, solid feature in the garden and can be used as part of a group or as a specimen plant.

ORIGIN Of garden origin.
MATURE HEIGHT 2m/7ft (10 years – 60cm/2ft).
SHAPE Conical.
LEAVES Golden changing to bright green. Held in the vertical plane.
CULTIVATION No problems in cultivation.
SITUATION Any size of garden.
HARDINESS Zone 5.

TSUGA (PINACEAE)
HEMLOCKS

This genus consists of ten or eleven species of large trees. They come from North America and throughout South and South East Asia. They derive their common name from the fact that the leaves, when crushed, smell the same as those of the herb hemlock, *Conium maculatum*. The hemlocks are closely related to the spruces, *Picea*. The foliage is flat and needlelike, each joined to the shoot by a short projection (shorter than in *Picea*). The wild trees are mainly quite large, but in cultivation there are many cultivars that are suitable for small gardens. They are not difficult to cultivate and make good garden plants, either as specimens or as hedging. The majority of the cultivars belong to *T. canadensis*.

TSUGA CANADENSIS 'MINIMA'
MINIMA HEMLOCK

This is a low, spreading hemlock that never grows to a great size. Its fresh-looking foliage is carried in flat sprays which gently overlap, like waves landing on a shore. It is the kind of plant that fits perfectly on the edge of a path or patio, particularly as a feature on a corner.
ORIGIN Of garden origin.
MATURE HEIGHT 90cm/1ft (10 years – 30cm/12in).
SHAPE Spreading.
LEAVES Light to mid-green, held in flat sprays.
CULTIVATION No problems in cultivation.
SITUATION Any size of garden, including large rock gardens.
HARDINESS Zone 5.

TSUGA CANADENSIS '*PENDULA*'
WEEPING HEMLOCK

This is a superb weeping conifer. The branches literally cascade down. It looks best if planted high on a rockery or on top of a retaining wall, where its branches are displayed to their best advantage. Alternatively, train one stem upward as a short trunk to, say, 90cm/3ft, and then allow the plant to cascade.

ORIGIN Of garden origin.

MATURE HEIGHT Depending on height of original training.

SHAPE Weeping or prostrate if untrained.

LEAVES Light to mid-green.

CULTIVATION Apart from the need to train if you want a taller plant, this shrub has no cultivation problems.

SITUATION Any size of garden, including large rock gardens.

HARDINESS Zone 5.

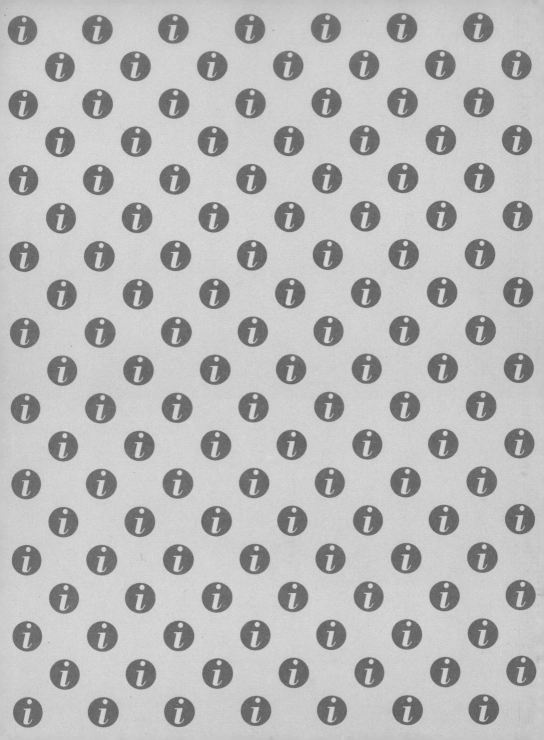